# Surviving Toxic Leaders

# Surviving Toxic Leaders

*How to Work for Flawed People in Churches, Schools, and Christian Organizations*

Kenneth O. Gangel

WIPF & STOCK · Eugene, Oregon

SURVIVING TOXIC LEADERS
How to Work for Flawed People in Churches, Schools, and Christian Organizations

Copyright © 2008 Kenneth O. Gangel. All rights reserved. Except for brief quotations in critical publications or reviews, no part of this book may be reproduced in any manner without prior written permission from the publisher. Write: Permissions, Wipf and Stock, 199 W. 8th Ave., Suite 3, Eugene, OR 97401.

ISBN 13: 978-1-55635-090-0

Manufactured in the U.S.A.

*This book was written for my son-in-law,
Timothy Gardner,
who has served more than enough time
under the abuse of toxic leaders.*

# Contents

*Foreword / ix*

*Acknowledgments / xi*

*Introduction / xiii*

1. What Is a Toxic Leader? / 1
2. It's Tough to Cheat a Cheater / 9
3. A New Pharaoh Has Arisen / 17
4. Time to Turn Off "American Idol" / 23
5. Incompetence Can Be Cured / 30
6. Ignorance Is Definitely Not Bliss! / 38
7. Cruel Leaders Are the Worst / 44
8. Bully for You! / 50
9. "It's My Way or the Highway" / 58
10. Sinking the Sloth / 64
11. Entering the Detox Lab / 70
12. Terminating Toxicity / 76

*Bibliography / 89*

# Foreword

## *Surviving Toxic Leaders*

Skull and Crossbones commonly warned an earlier generation away from poisoned wells on the American frontier and bottles of Iodine in the family medicine cabinet. Next came Mr. Ick with his ugly face discouraging children from household cleansers in the kitchen and garden pesticides in the garage. Now there are caution labels on dangerous products and instructions to immediately call 911 if contaminated. These are all warnings against the poisons that can blind our eyes, burn our skin, damage our brains and take our lives.

Ironically, most warning labels are on products intended to do good. But good intentions do not guarantee protection from poisoning.

Churches and other Christian organizations aren't pasted with warning labels but toxins too often abound. Maybe the dangers are greater at church because our guard is down and our expectations are up. We assume that Christian leaders are good people with pure motives and healthy souls. Going to church is like going to a health food store where toxins are never allowed.

Well, just as health food stores can't keep toxins out and hospitals can give you a staph infection, so churches and their leaders are not exempt from bad leadership. Just as there were toxic leaders in the Bible there are toxic leaders in twenty-first century churches. So, what should we do? Here's the short list:

1. Seek health—God loves a healthy church and so should we.
2. Watch out—keep eyes wide open for toxic church leadership.
3. Take action—run from the poison; take the antidote; call for help.

Now for the long list. Kenn Gangel brings a lifetime of leadership studies, a warm and broad knowledge of the Bible and personal encounters with thousands of Christian leaders. He adds an amazing familiarity with leadership literature. He puts all this together in a guidebook for both leaders

*Foreword*

and followers who are cautious enough to avoid the dangers, courageous enough to confront the poisons, and committed enough to build healthy churches and Christian organizations for our generation.

Leith Anderson<br>
President, National Association of Evangelicals<br>
Pastor, Wooddale Church<br>
July 3, 2007

# Acknowledgments

For nearly 20 years Mrs. Ginny Murray has been typing manuscripts for me. First as my administrative assistant at Dallas Seminary, and later on a free-lance basis. Her faithfulness and attentiveness has been a great blessing and I know she types every word as a service to her Lord. In addition, Mrs. Denise Speed has also contributed much to the preparation of this book, and my wife of over 50 years, Betty Gangel, reads and provides helpful comments on all my work, now 57 books worth. I thank God for all three.

# Introduction

WE ALL say that people are the most important part of our organizations, yet too many leaders treat people as profit or loss lines on the accounting statement. Even in churches, lay leaders are often "used" by professional leaders to achieve the goals and ends of the latter. Such behavior results in anger, leaving the church, and a spirit of bitterness throughout the congregation or organization.

This book makes clear that we face the problem of toxic leadership in the church at a very real and present level, yet over 90% of the pastors, elders and deacons in North America will not read Lipman-Blumen's work nor see this one either, so the diseases created by toxicity persist.

Recently a pastor said to me about a growing church in his area, "I wish I could get a template of what they do and impose it on my church." He bristled slightly at my response: "That might be the worst possible scenario for the future of your ministry here." No one develops authenticity in leadership by imitating someone else. No one develops credibility by abusing someone else. You can learn from others' experiences, but there is no way you can be successful when you are trying to be like them.

Stanford Graduate School of Business has an advisory council made up of 75 distinguished people. Each of them were asked to recommend the most important capability for leaders to develop. They unanimously chose self-awareness. In other words, if you are in a state of abuse because of a toxic leader you need to know that. And if you are abusing others as a toxic leader you need to understand that as well.

That's what this book will help you do. We will take a look at the nature of toxicity, especially in Christian ministry, and specifically identify several types of toxic behavior and how one can survive those behaviors.

The reality of toxicity exists because both knowledge and power are dispersed widely in any effective organization. Decision-making then, far removed from the desks of the top executives alone, spans multiple levels and proceeds on parallel yet independent tracks. But decision-making is only one way of recognizing toxicity, though it may be the very best. Our focus throughout this book centers not just on tuning up your church or suggesting ways to help it run better, it directly targets looking at bibli-

*Introduction*

cal examples of toxicity and applying those lessons of God's Word to the behaviors we have come to know and to live out in the church.

Kenneth O. Gangel<br>
Toccoa Falls, Georgia

# 1

# What Is a Toxic Leader?

A VAST percentage of leadership books in both the secular and religious domains deal with how to move from average to good or good to great in your own leadership, or how to help other people on your team do just that. The same analysis holds true in periodical literature, both journals and magazines. That's why Jean Lipman-Blumen's book hit the market with a crash in 2004. The title alone suggests, one could say, an "alluring" analysis of something we have swept into the corner and refused to look at: *The Allure of Toxic Leaders: Why We Follow Destructive Bosses and Corrupt Politicians—and How We Can Survive Them.*

Defective Christian leaders rarely get their pictures in *Time* or *Newsweek* for defrauding employees or driving their ministries into bankruptcy, but make no mistake about it, we have toxic leaders in our midst. Lipman-Blumen wonders why people follow such leaders and decides they do so because of a desire for dependence, a need to play a more crucial role in the organization, and just plain fear.

In strong prose, she reminds us that "fixing" toxic leaders is not often an option. Perhaps a strong group of key opinion-shapers within the organization should *confront and counsel them*. She also suggests quietly working *to undermine the leader* or perhaps even joining with others to overtly *overthrow the leader*. I have serious doubts that the latter two would advance any Christian organization. What allows abused leaders to survive, sometimes even thrive? There must be a "buffering sufferer" who takes the sting from the top and softens it for those below. Middle management leaders can protect their people and make it possible for them to effectively carry out their work undeterred by storms at the top.

But that stop-gap solution might not always work. We must understand the biblical and spiritual consequences of toxic leadership and attempt to at least cut the percentage of toxic leaders in the ranks of evangelical ministries. That's what this book can do. But first we have to begin with an understanding of the concept of toxic leadership. To be sure, toxic leaders are better described than defined, but *toxicity* is a clear term in the

English language and I believe we can make the necessary crossover from the field of medicine to our understanding of leadership. So let me introduce my expert, *The American Heritage Dictionary of the English Language* published by the good folks at Houghton Mifflin Company with offices in Boston and New York (3rd edition).

The adjective *toxic* means "of, relating to, or caused by a toxin or other poison: . . . capable of causing injury or death." The word comes from the late Latin *toxicus* and from the Greek *toxikon*, both meaning poison. The noun *toxicity* simply means "the quality or condition of being toxic." The noun *toxin* describes "a poisonous substance, especially a protein, produced by living cells or organisms, capable of causing disease when introduced into the body tissues but often also capable of inducing neutralizing antibodies or antitoxins" (1,895). We could go on, but you get the idea. Toxicity often appears in connection with snake venom, alcohol, or fallout in the environment from the mishandling of heavy metals such as lead, or solvents such as carbon tetrachloride.

## Characteristics of a Toxic Leader

I have already mentioned a few of these above in my brief allusion to the work of Lipman-Blumen but the list of characteristics seems almost longer than we can treat. Furthermore, the complex blend of these personality traits in toxic leaders renders it impossible to pinpoint the exact problem through which the leader injects poison into the organization. The best we can do is acknowledge the presence of a toxic leader, then make an attempt to deal with it in whatever way available to us at the time. So let me list ten qualities commonly found in toxic leaders in one or more blends, and then deal with each one separately in its own chapter. By the way, I intend no severity growing or declining throughout this list. These are separate entities, each one no less or no more dangerous to ministry than the others.

### *The Deceptive Leader*

For this character trait we need no long sessions of debate or discussion; Scripture provides the perfect example in the third patriarch, Jacob. Surprised? The very fact that some readers thought I would start listing people like Hitler, Mussolini, Mao TseTung, or Saddam Hussein indicates already that we have the wrong concept of toxicity. A person with toxins in his or her body does not necessarily feel those toxins nor know their origin. If you have just been bitten by a Copperhead and you can clearly identify the snake to medical authorities, there is no guessing involved.

But if you just go home night after night with a migraine headache and no physical cause can be found, you might be working for a toxic leader and, sometimes, the toxicity might be deception.

## *The Autocratic Leader*

Leaders given to total control of an organization, micro-managers, dictators, operate that way largely because they have an overly-developed ambition, or perhaps an inappropriate or inordinate ambition. This might be the most common kind of toxic leader in Christian organizations because they can hide behind the authority of ordination, office, or even a particular interpretation of Scripture. They warn you and other members of the staff not to "touch the Lord's anointed" lest God bring some destructive horror into your life.

## *The Egotistic Leader*

Those familiar with the literature on leadership studies know that virtually every expert indicates leaders must have some touch of ego in order to take the point position and hold it through sun and storm. But let's not confuse pride of workmanship with flat out arrogance.

## *The Incompetent Leader*

People in a subordinate relationship find it most difficult to harbor the nagging thought that the boss might not know as much about their jobs as they do. I've spent a good part of my life working with students who graduated and enter assistant or associate positions in churches and other organizations. In some cases they walk into ideal learning situations in which a veteran pastor full of wisdom can help them through the rocky early years. In others however, they sign on with a church cursed by a leadership vacuum in which there exists a "Judges-like atmosphere," people doing that which seems right in their own eyes.

## *The Ignorant Leader*

A fine line exists between *incompetence* and *ignorance*. An incompetent leader simply does not know what to do. The ignorant leader simply does not know anything about leadership. He might be a walking encyclopedia in other areas, but incapable of understanding the specific arena of leadership. That explains why many faculty cannot function as administrators.

## *The Cruel Leader*

As indicated earlier, our minds immediately dance to this tune when we think about a word as nasty as *toxicity* in relation to Christian leaders. But thousands of people have seen cruel leaders in operation and still suffer the effects. I never fell into the curse of working for a cruel leader, but I did live with a cruel father during the earliest years of my life, so I have some personal sense of this disease.

## *The Evil Leader*

Some leaders simply lack integrity and authenticity regardless of their titles. Have we not seen world renowned pastors and television evangelists fall into adultery or theft with some regularity over the last several decades? Furthermore, evil leaders frequently come by their positions circuitously or even violently so their followers operate in fear right from the beginning. We'll have to take a close look at this one.

## *The Demanding Leader*

Almost all autocrats or cruel leaders are demanding, but not every demanding leader practices either cruel or autocratic leadership. In this chapter we will focus on the so-called "perfectionists" who cannot stand errors in their own lives and ministries and therefore will not tolerate them in others. To be sure, one can more easily work with this person than some of the others, but the toxicity that emanates from such an environment destroys the team spirit we all want to develop in our organizations. Teams thrive on shared commitment. Without it, people perform as individuals; with it, they become a powerful unit of collective performance.

In every effective team, the members genuinely agree to become accountable with and to their teammates. The dynamic that keeps arising here notes that a working group depends on the performance of individuals, but an effective team is always worth more than the sum of its parts. Leaders who foster team development in the right place at the right time prime their organizations for top performance. As Katzenbach and Smith once wrote in the *Harvard Business Review*, "The difference between teams that perform and other groups that don't is a subject to which most of us pay far too little attention."[1]

---

1. Katzenbach and Smith, 162.

### *The Reckless Leader*

I'm tempted to say here that one can spot reckless leaders most clearly by laziness, but we know of many other forms of recklessness. We all find it difficult to serve lazy leaders if we are aggressive and eager to get the job done. But recklessness or carelessness can introduce toxicity to any organization. Titus learned this first hand about two thousand years ago and we can profit from his experience.

## Why Would People Work for a Toxic Leader?

With the stench of the Enron disaster still in our nostrils, we have become accustomed to the ongoing lawsuits from employees who lost everything. Let's remember that most of the people who left Enron didn't drop out or voluntarily go to other businesses. They actually loved their jobs and felt they functioned at the center of action in such a gigantic corporation. But clearly toxic leadership ruled at Enron, so why did people stay?

### *Belief in the Unbelievable*

The old wisdom says when something looks too good to be true it probably is. Stock portfolios, retirement packages, working conditions—everything seemed right and most of Enron's people felt they were functioning in one of the greatest companies ever built. That's why pastors are less likely to leave a large church than a small one. However, a large organization affords part of the draw for an autocratic toxic leader who needs full command until someone blows the whistle.

### *Following the Illusion*

Leaders too smart to believe in the unbelievable might fail to descern the descriptions and analyses that toxic leaders communicate to their people. Toxic leaders may not be as harmless as doves, but they are often as smart as serpents. They create illusions of achievement and great hope for the future "If you just stick with me." We are, after all, an idol-worshiping people who glorify their heroes and heap riches upon them; why wouldn't we follow a leader in charge of some great business or ministry?

### *Desire for Dependence*

Some may recognize Lipman-Blumen's words. When asked why people follow or work for a toxic leader, she talks first about the *myth of independence* which still permeates a country that lost its independence to bureaucracy some time during the twentieth century. The colonial patriots whose iron will and willingness to die for what they believed has given way to a shabby antinomian society willing to put up with the worst kind of immorality as long as they themselves are protected, fed and cared for.

### *Fear*

Again, one of Lipman-Blumen's answers when asked why people would work for a toxic leader. In one interview she refers to Harold Geneen of IT&T where employees were so frightened of the boss they became physically ill and couldn't sleep for nights before they needed to report to him. Toxic leaders do not dispel such fear, they encourage it.

### *No Other Options*

Sometimes we simply cannot find a way out. That applies to people in ministry as well as people in business organizations. A single mom without a college degree may be required to hold on to her secretarial job even though the boss behaves like a monster. We will have to deal with this seemingly hopeless dilemma before the book ends.

## How Toxic Leaders Create Toxic Organizations

Definitions loom important here, and fortunately, not difficult to identify. Robert Bacal defines toxic organizations in a useful three category model: "We can think of organizations as falling on a continuum. One end is anchored by organizations that function well. In the middle we find the average organization that is effective but could be better. Finally we have the toxic organization, an organization that is largely ineffective, but is also destructive to its employees and leaders."[2]

Bacal gets much more specific when he begins to identify the characteristics that mark a toxic organization as different from a healthy organization. For example, a toxic organization has a history of poor performance—*it does not fulfill its mission, it does not achieve its goals, it does not do what it claims it will do.*

Leading the parade to poor performance we usually find ineffective decision-making. I've often told doctoral students in leadership classes that an analysis of decision-making has become my primary way to analyze an organization, company or ministry. A team-centered ministry

---

2. Bacal, "Welcome to the Fire of an Unhealthy Workplace," 1.

will immediately display genuine group decision-making as opposed to advisory groups who say what they wish and then leave the decision to a single leader. This remains one of the most misunderstood aspects of effective leadership.

We also recognize a toxic organization by its high levels of dissatisfaction and stress. These result from destructive human relations not unlike the relationships we see in dysfunctional families. People get discouraged, good people leave the organization, but somehow, things just don't seem to improve. So we can specify so far that toxic organizations are:

- Helpless in making things better
- Not supportive emotionally or professionally
- Unable to identify the causes of the discomfort and pain
- Unable to leave the situation permanently and unable to solve problems permanently
- Consistently under attack[3]

We have already noted that a toxic organization does not fulfill its mission, so we should go on to say that it has virtually no capacity to handle serious problem-solving. Its whole climate militates against the kind of relationships essential for handling problems—poor communication, bad decision-making, and manipulative, self-centered leaders.

Bacal gets even more specific.

> The toxic organization is most often a relatively small work unit where there is considerable face-to-face interaction among the work unit members. This is because inter-personal relationships stand at the core of the sick organization. If there is a low level of interaction, it is likely that a toxic organization will emerge.[4]

At the top of this pyramid are managers who tend to be cold and distant, sometimes deliberately so. Toxic managers avoid people and situations that may require explanation of their decisions or behavior. Whether or not she knows why she behaves as she does, the toxic manager confuses subordinates, thereby reducing the trust level and increasing the fear of punishment or failure.

Dan Chenoweth talks about the possibility of turning the situation around, obviously the intent of this entire book.

---

3. Ibid., 2
4. Ibid.

One positive result of such a process is that the entire organization is impacted when anyone in a leadership role becomes humble and open to core changes. If you are the person that spotted the bully behavior and took action toward intervention, you may feel an incredible personal sense of reward. You may see yourself as a key player in the evolution of the human spirit of your company, and in its advancement toward a more sustainable "human" culture that truly values learning, cooperation, and collaboration. Handing leadership development "crutches" to a "broken" leader can be the greatest gift you could ever give to that individual—and to your entire organization.[5]

## Stopping Toxic Leaders

Chenoweth has already given us a great start on this but let's take the point just a bit further. Since toxic leaders thrive on the vulnerability of poor and ignorant people; they create fantasies and illusions which seem to the people who follow them as reality. Stagnation and mediocrity characterize their organizations and leadership, in the best sense of the word, is virtually invisible. Vincent L. Ferguson in his article "Stopping Toxic Leaders" reworks Lipman-Blumen's advice.

> As we seek the leadership capacity in ourselves, we should work cdaciously at strengthening our democratic institutions. We must, suggests Ms. Lipman-Blumen, throw out the passive obedience role to which the toxic leaders have assigned us, patiently avoiding directives. We, after all, were made to be thinking, feeling beings with varying leadership capacities, which are not meant to be hidden under a basket. Organizational society can only become stronger and more vibrant when we try to pursue our potential as our Creator intended.[6]

---

5. Chenoweth, "Five Characteristics That Differentiate Great Leaders from Toxic Leaders," 2
6. Ferguson, "Stopping Toxic Leaders," 2.

2

# It's Tough to Cheat a Cheater

W. J. McCalkin lived a wealthy but irritated life. Determined to send his children to a Christian school, he became very upset upon discovering that none existed in his area, so he decided to build one. Not to start one, but to build one. He bought a piece of land, had a building erected with several classrooms, and opened the doors.

After about two years McCalkin noticed that the growth factor seemed to slow down even though the school did not yet have 100 students. He had named himself chairman of the board and selected other board members, so in every sense this was what educators call a "proprietary institution." Wisely, he and the other board members decided to search for a principal. They contacted a Christian graduate school nearby and hired the first candidate they interviewed. The new principal had approximately ten years experience in the classroom and two years internship in administration, as well as a Master's degree in Educational Administration.

Oila! A perfect marriage. The school began to grow; the parents were excited; the upper half of the building was completed and almost immediately filled—one would think McCalkin's dream had come true.

But a subtle change took place along the way. The new principal (we'll call him Sam), because of his everyday presence among the students and at all parental events, logically became the head of the school, something McCalkin had not figured into the equation. No one was at fault. It would be highly unusual in any school for parents and students to think of the Chairman of the Board rather than the principal as the chief leader of the school.

At the very point he felt those pangs of jealousy, McCalkin could have talked with Sam irenically and worked out some kind of satisfactory compromise. Instead, he said nothing, while deceptively planning behind the principal's back to attack him one day off campus with a portion of the board and tell him he must resign immediately. So immediately, in fact, that they locked his office door and he could not return to the building to gather his own belongings. In all the stories I have heard about education in over fifty years, this represents the most blatant case of jealousy and deceptiveness at any level of schooling.

One could argue that Sam never worked for a deceptive leader since he never really had a chance to deal with the problem, being fired "on the spot," so to speak. But that's not true. He had worked for a deceptive leader, probably for months. Whether he sensed a problem or not; whether any board discussions drifted in this direction or not; whether gossip spread among the constituency or not—the school imploded from the underhanded work of a deceptive leader.

## The Great Deceiver

Typical bitter, angry song lyrics of the twenty-first century too accurately describe the hearts of deceiving leaders. Nevertheless, deception has been a part of human relations for thousands of years. During the days of the patriarchs nepotism ruled the marriage patterns, so after Jacob had deceived his father Isaac to gain the family blessing and birthright, his mother sent him away to live with his Uncle Laban. You remember that Jacob was the son of Rebekah and Isaac. His grandfather Abraham had a brother Nahor, grandfather to Laban.

This means that Jacob related to Laban in three ways: through his grandfather Abraham; through his mother Rebekah, Laban's sister; and through marriage when Laban became his father-in-law. To simply say "Jacob worked for his uncle" does not capture all the nuances of this tri-polar relationship. Jacob had already made a covenant with God and surely thought his life had a new start when he met and loved Rachel, working seven years for her hand in marriage.

No one likes to be lied to or deceived, but when such things happen on one's wedding night, the problem gets considerably more complicated. And the disasters just multiply—Rachel envies her sister Leah because of her seven children; Leah becomes jealous of Rachel because of her beauty; Jacob favored Rachel's sons Joseph and Benjamin, thereby driving his other ten sons away from family loyalty. They ultimately sold their own brother into slavery. No, there could not be a better example anywhere of working for a deceptive boss than Jacob out in Laban's fields.

When Jacob finally decided to leave at the end of fourteen years, Laban upped the ante and offered to pay Jacob whatever he asked. Jacob already had descendents, now he would like a piece of the prosperity. If we were reading contemporary fiction here, we would anticipate that Laban had some scheme in his pocket to outwit Jacob again. For these two, one-upmanship was a way of life.

The Bible reader understands, (and Jacob knew) that the outcome of whatever happened with the flocks and herds God had determined. But Laban never got that far. He assumed that if any good would come into his life, he had to make it happen, even if it meant lying and deceiving other people. His entire demeanor consistently characterizes a toxic boss.

Some years ago I authored a commentary on the book of Genesis and included the following paragraphs comparing Jacob to the current problems of post-modernism:

> Some would argue that the first 21st century enemy of absolute truth is the spirit of post-modernism which began to build in the late 1900s. Among its other characteristics, post-modernism abandons absolute truth, preferring to create its own truth and approaching virtually every subject with free-lance subjectivism. Christians believe that absolute truth is discovered in the absolute Word of God. Postmodernists believe truth is designed or created, and therefore, what is true for one person may not be true for another, nor must truth synchronize with reality or rationality.

In his famous book *The Closing of the American Mind*, Alan Bloom complained that post-modern university students fear the danger of absolutism because it carries with it the ultimate curse—intolerance. He argues that virtually every entering college freshman is sure of one thing—all truth is relative.

> At this point in his life, Jacob struggled with absolutes, attempting to engineer his world by his own schemes. After all, until he met Laban, it had always worked. Now maybe the old magic had returned. Although he mentioned God at various times, he hardly had a handle on sovereignty and still apparently believed he controlled his own destiny and that of his family.[1]

## What Deception Does to a Leader

Like Mr. McCalkin, Laban was a wealthy man, and also like Mr. McCalkin, he considered it his right to manipulate everyone around him. Let's not forget that in this story both Jacob and Laban regularly practice deception, in fact, both were world-class deceivers. Jacob labored in Paddan Aram for twenty years, fourteen for his wives, and six earning wages and

---

1. Gangel and Bramer, *Genesis*, 253–54.

increasing his own herds and flocks. When he left he had eleven sons and one daughter and still feared his brother Esau who had threatened his death—but that's another story. As the grandson of Abraham he may not have completely understood the patriarchal promise program, but he surely knew that God expected him to exercise leadership like his father and grandfather. However, the Genesis account indicates that the quality of leadership deteriorated significantly from generation to generation, and Jacob barely maintained any credibility when it appeared his family would starve in Canaan.

What might Jacob have done that he didn't do? Spiritually, Jacob was simply a late bloomer. We think that the wrestling match the night before he met Esau (Genesis 32) may have been a turning point except that the story of Dinah and the Shechemites follows, then the story of Esau's improper marriage, and finally, the feud among the brothers. One passage prior to the famous wrestling match indicates a prayer genuinely biblical, humble and dependent on God.

> Then Jacob prayed, "O God of my father Abraham, God of my father Isaac, O Lord, who said to me, 'Go back to your country and your relatives, and I will make you prosper,' I am unworthy of all the kindness and faithfulness you have shown your servant. I had only my staff when I crossed the Jordan, but now I have become two groups. Save me, I pray, from the hand of my brother Esau, for I am afraid he will come and attack me, and also the mothers with their children. But you have said, 'I will surely make you prosper and will make your descendants like the sand of the sea, which cannot be counted.'" (Gen 32:9–12)

Jacob lived very differently from Abraham and Isaac. He learned new forms of leadership to cope with the strange situations in which he repeatedly found himself.

David Dotlich and Peter Cairo, the founding partners of the executive development firm CDR, International, talk about learning leadership approaches which are "unnatural"; in fact, they entitle their book *Unnatural Leadership*. They identify "10 Unnatural Acts" that most effective leaders regularly commit, considered unnatural because they are appropriate responses to an irrational, chaotic and unpredictable world.

- Refuse to be a prisoner of experience
- Expose your vulnerabilities
- Acknowledge your shadow side

- Develop a right-versus-right decision-making mentality
- Create teams that create discomfort
- Trust others before they earn it
- Coach and teach as well as lead and inspire
- Connect instead of create
- Give up some control
- Challenge the conventional wisdom[2]

With the possible exception of trusting Laban for seven years before that conniver had earned anyone's trust, Jacob fails virtually every other point in this list.

Notice Dotlich and Cairo call for a *positive response to negative surroundings*. Jacob eventually came around to that for a while, but then fell away again to his deceiving self. In this behavior he illustrates for us how easily a deceiver can be deceived. As late as Genesis 37 he buys into the story of Joseph's death by "some ferocious animal" (37:33). Michael Useem, Director of the Center for Leadership and Change at the Wharton School, says, "Leadership has always required more than a downward touch. It needs to come from below as well as above, and leaders today must reach up not just down."[3]

## What Deception Does to a Team

Part of the allure of this particular toxicity is what Donald Trump might call "the challenge of the deal." Laban's behavior never depresses Jacob though it creates problems in his life for over two decades. He acts as though this is the normal way of doing business and enters readily into the "I'll get you before you can get me" syndrome. That kind of attitude can settle like a cloud of gloom over an entire organization or ministry. But let's get even more specific.

---

2. Dotlich and Cairo, *Unnatural Leadership*, 17.
3. Useem, "How Well-Run Boards Make Decisions," 130.

## *Deception Causes Leaders to Ignore God's Providence and Protection*

Both Jacob and Laban repeatedly illustrate their self dependence. Interestingly, the word *providence* does not occur in the Bible but it represents a genuine biblical doctrine. There is no single Hebrew word that we can translate as *providence*. The Greek word *pronoia* seems to describe human foresight (Acts 24:2; Rom 13:14). The doctrine of providence becomes the stage on which the drama of Genesis is played out. It deals with God's gracious outworking of His plan in the lives of His people, and ultimately in the salvation story of Christ and the Cross.

> If we only had Genesis 30 without 31, we would imagine Jacob constructing some kind of magic formula to enhance his flocks. But chapter 31 shows us that all the success of Jacob's experiments depended upon God.
>
> God's providence even orchestrates negative human emotions and actions to achieve His purposes. As the jealousy of Jacob's wives led to the birth of the tribes of Israel, so the jealousy of Laban and his sons led to Jacob's return to the land of his fathers. The folly of Rachel in stealing the household gods enabled Jacob to win his lawsuit.
>
> Belief in the providence of God reminds us that the entire world and our individual lives are not determined by chance or fate but by God and His purposes, often being worked out behind the scenes.[4]

## *Deception Ruins Trust*

Repeatedly in my classes and books I have emphasized trust as a major, perhaps *the* primary leadership ingredient. People cannot follow someone they do not trust. But trust works two ways. Leaders generally do not release authority and responsibility to people whose credibility for competence and reliability may be shaky. We enhance team relationships when we distribute leadership across the organization and provide empowerment to others.

Everything we say about the credibility and capability of leaders applies to the work and ministry of creative followers, in most cases themselves. Dave Ulrich says that all leaders should be "less concerned with saying what they will deliver and more concerned with delivering what

---

4. Gangel and Bramer, *Genesis*, 270.

they have said they would. . . . Consistent, reliable, predictable delivery on promises [forms] the foundation of leadership."[5]

## *Deception Divides Teams and Families*

The division of Abraham's family has never been more prominent than it is in the twenty-first century. What began as Abraham's mating with Sarah's Egyptian servant girl to produce Ishmael (the first Arab) plays out in all news media pieces on the Middle East everyday of our lives. In Jacob's case, as the remainder of the book of Genesis unfolds, we see breakdown after breakdown in his family.

Exactly the same thing happens in organizations. Here we see one of most toxic leaders' favorite tools. If they can break up the team, playing factions against one another, they then hold the high ground, or so it appears. Lipman-Blumen says that people are willing to follow untrustworthy leaders because

> We live in such an unfinished and unfinishable world, where today's knowledge is unraveled and respun by new discoveries, demanding still newer knowledge and newer discoveries. This unfinished and unfinishable world confronts us with limitless challenges in each new era, setting and resetting the stage for heroic action.[6]

## *Deceptive Leaders Create an Atmosphere of Paranoia*

We talked about fear in chapter 1 because some fears are normal in any workplace—fear of not getting along with other people, fear of failure, fear of being criticized, and so on. But *paranoia* arises as a much stronger word which refers to a psychotic disorder characterized by illusions of persecution or grandeur, often strenuously defended with apparent logic and reason. So here we see that the toxic leader not only creates fear, but she herself operates from a position of paranoia, namely, the possibility of losing power. Paranoia then paralyzes the organization and what results is a group of people working under the same roof or on the same property, day after day, who cannot achieve operational goals, cannot talk to one another in terms that will advance the mission, and cannot retain a team perspective. Each pursues his or her own agenda, and over all this hovers a cloud of hopelessness. *Toxic organizations do not tend to believe they can get better.*

5. Ulrich, "Credibility X Capability."
6. Lipman-Blumen. "Toxic Leadership," 31.

# Christmas in April

Robert Morgan chose the title "Christmas in April" to describe the ministry of Christmas Evans, a Welch evangelist born on December 25, 1776, to a poor shoemaker and his wife. When Evans was nine, his father died in the cobbler stall. Christmas ended up in the home of an alcoholic uncle. Through the preaching of David Davies, Christmas gave his life to Christ and began to learn Scripture by candlelight at a barn in Penyralltfawr. The wild gang he had been running with was so upset by his conversion and calling to preach that they beat him and gouged out his right eye. As Morgan tells the story,

> The young man resolved nonetheless to preach, and preach he did. Wherever he went—churches, coal mines, open fields—crowds gathered and a spirit of revival swept over the listeners. Unable to afford a horse, he started across Wales by foot, preaching in towns and villages with great effect.
>
> On April 10, 1802, Evans, having burned out in ministry and lost the joy of the Lord, climbed into the Welsh mountains to pray until God brought revival to his heart. He made a covenant with God that day, writing down thirteen items, initialing each one. The fourth said, "Grant that I may not be left to any foolish act that may occasion my gifts to wither." The eighth said, "Grant that I may experience the power of Thy word before I deliver it."[7]

Evans came down from the mountain like Moses and rumbled through Wales and the neighboring island of Angeles for the next 36 years. Some historians still refer to him as "The Bunyan of Wales." No deception in that kind of life; *leaders with integrity keep the mission foremost.*

---

7. Morgan, "April 10," *On This Day*, 3.

# 3

# A New Pharaoh Has Arisen

Some leaders make the people around them nervous and stressed out simply because of their inordinate or overdeveloped ambition. Obviously ambition is a positive trait and being ambitious does not make a person a toxic leader. But when that ambition gets out of hand, minimizing the mission and trampling on the team, we have crossed over into autocracy as a primary leadership style.

In my seven previously published leadership books, I have said in one way or another that leaders must understand how to intentionally select a leadership style. I have also tried to emphasize that dealing with leadership style can be reasonably simple or hugely complex. The simplest form is shown in the diagram below. Autocratic leaders (full personal control by the main leader) fall to the extreme right of the diagram and "free rein" leadership ("hands off" approach to dealing with the team) to the left. Dead in the middle we find team leadership, or what we called twenty years ago, "participatory leadership."

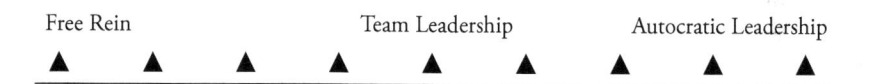

| Free Rein | Team Leadership | Autocratic Leadership |
|---|---|---|
| ▲　▲　▲ | ▲　▲　▲ | ▲　▲　▲ |

Some may ask, "I have heard a lot about *servant-leadership*; how is that different from team leadership?" That all depends what a person perceives by the concept of *servant leadership*. Because of the work of Robert K. Greenleaf such terminology is widely used in secular areas. Larry Spears tells us, "The term *servant leadership* was first coined by Greenleaf (1904–1999) in a 1970 essay entitled 'The Servant as Leaders.'"[1] He goes on to say

> The idea of the servant as leader came partly out of Greenleaf's half-century of experience in working to shape large institutions.

1. Spears, *Leader to Leader*, 7.

However, the event that crystallized Greenleaf's thinking came in the 1960s when he read Hermann Hesse's short novel *Journey to the East*—an account of a mythical journey by a group of people on a spiritual quest.[2]

In fact, the true concept of servant leadership goes considerably back beyond Greenleaf or Hesse, all the way to Jesus who repeatedly taught His disciples the concept of servant leadership (Luke 22:24–26; Mark 9:33–35). As Spears goes on to identify what he considers to be the qualities of servant leadership, he includes listening, empathy, healing, awareness, persuasion, conceptualization, foresight, stewardship, commitment to groups of people, and building community. But he is completely right when he adds, "These ten characteristics of servant-leadership are by no means exhaustive, but they serve to communicate the power and promise that this concept offers to those who are open to its invitation and challenge."[3]

For those serving in Christian ministry of any kind, servant leadership is a biblically mandated and prescribed form of behavior which requires one to work with his or her colleagues as a compatible, loving, and caring team in order to achieve the ends God wishes to attain in that ministry. "Being ambitious for God" holds no wrong except that people with sinful natures almost always tend to over-extend that ambition and eventually focus on themselves rather than on the ministry or the Master.

Suffice it to say that every source I have cited in the first two chapters (and many I have not cited) all use words such as *extremely unethical, amoral, lacking credibility, politically astute, maladjusted, malicious,* and *cleverness at concealing deceit.* Marsha Whicker claims

> They succeed by tearing others down. They glory in turf protection, fighting, and controlling others rather than uplifting followers. They are "red light" leaders who destroy productivity and apply brakes to organizational progress. . . . Three types of toxic leaders are enforcers, street fighters, and bullies.[4]

## How Ambition Creates Toxicity

We need only move from Jacob to his son Joseph in order to find rampant ambition in two leaders, both of whom Joseph had to call "boss." When the Ishmaelite nomads reached Egypt they sold Joseph to Potiphar, captain

---

2. Ibid., 8.
3. Ibid., 10.
4. Whicker, *When Organizations Go Bad,* 27.

of the body guard who almost immediately made Joseph steward of his house. Potiphar held ultimate responsibility for Pharaoh's life, had charge of all important prisoners, and often required to pass judgment of execution. Joseph's gifts in administration immediately propelled him to Head of Household which obviously brought him in contact with Potiphar's wife who found him more than generally attractive.

Note that Joseph's faithfulness to God, not his fear of prison or hesitation to violate social custom, required him to turn down her seductions. We find one of the great leadership passages in the Bible in Genesis 39:8–9.

> But he refused. "With me in charge," he told her, "my master does not concern himself with anything in the house; everything he owns he has entrusted to my care. No one is greater in this house than I am. My master has withheld nothing from me except you, because you are his wife. How then could I do such a wicked thing and sin against God?" (Gen 39:8–9).

But Joseph hadn't seen anything yet. Released from prison he gets catapulted to the level of prime minister after interpreting Pharaoh's dream. Gil Beers puts it this way:

> Joseph was second-in-command over the entire land of Egypt. Only Pharaoh himself had more power and authority. Pharaoh had great trust in Joseph, for he told the people to do whatever Joseph asked (Gen 41:55). Joseph may have been in charge of Egypt's army, finances, agriculture, and justice system.[5]

Working for a toxic leader is not much fun whether in Potiphar's house, prison or politics. Of course, we cannot be sure that Joseph himself did not become an autocratic leader in Egypt, though the compassion he shows for his wicked brothers and his father demonstrate a completely changed heart. My co-author of the Genesis commentary mentioned earlier, tells us more about Joseph's situation in Egypt.

> Some scholars object to the idea that Joseph, a Semite and not an Egyptian, should be elevated to such a position in Egypt. But an Amarna letter (one of a series of letters written by Canaanite scribes detailing the relationship between Canaan and Egypt) dating from the fourteenth century BC has been discovered which possibly sheds light on such a practice. This letter was written to a person in a similar position with the Semite name of DuDu (or TuTu). He was appointed "Highest Mouth in the whole country."

---

5. Beers, *The Victor Handbook of Bible Knowledge*, 82.

So to be a Semite and to have a position of significant power is confirmed both within and outside of Scripture.[6]

## "Helping People Establish Their Goals"

The title of our third section appears in quotations because the words are not mine but rather adopted straight from an article by Marshall Goldsmith, recently named by the AMA as one of the fifty great thinkers and leaders in the field of management over the past eighty years. Everything I have ever read from his fertile mind has helped me better understand the intricacies of the leadership role. After observing that too rarely do we achieve organizational goals, he tells us "Six primary reasons explain why people give up on goals. Understanding these roadblocks to goal achievement can help you apply a little "preventive" medicine as you help others set goals—so ultimately they will be more likely to achieve their objectives for change."[7]

So Goldsmith reminds us that great leaders do not themselves set and achieve goals but rather assist the team in doing so. The first problem he deals with is that *people rarely take genuine ownership of their goals.*

> They assume that what leaders tell them will improve their work habits has little likelihood of success and when it fails they simply say, "that is exactly what I expected." The key here is to make sure people understand they are ultimately responsible for their own behavior.

The second issue is *time*. Goldsmith says, "In helping others set goals, it is important for them to be realistic about the time required to produce a positive, long-term change in behavior."[8] The third hurdle is *difficulty*. Leaders who make it sound simple to change one's pattern of behavior merely place another stumbling block in the paths of their colleagues. The issue in changing leadership behavior is not understanding but actually doing. Problem number four Goldsmith calls *distractions*: "In planning for the future, coaches need to help goal setters assume that unexpected distractions and competing goals will occur. Leaders should expect the unexpected and build in time to deal with it."[9]

---

6. Gangel and Bramer, *Genesis*, 340.
7. Goldsmith, *Leader to Leader*, 25.
8. Ibid., 26.
9. Ibid., 27.

*Rewards* claim fifth place because people get disappointed when all achievement doesn't seem to bring immediate benefit. Goldsmith hits the bull's eye when he argues, "Leaders need to understand that leadership is a *process*—not a *state*. Leaders can never 'get there.' Leaders are 'always getting there.' The only way exercise helps people stay in shape is when they face reality: 'I have to work on this stuff for the rest of my life!'"[10]

So autocrats, because of their overdeveloped and manipulative ambition, take over the decision-making and goal-setting processes of an organization and people abandon their own responsibilities and minimize the commitment required to reach ministry goals.

## "To the Third and Fourth Generation"

Max Dukes did not believe in Christ or in Christian training. He refused to take his children to church even when they asked to go. He has had 1,026 descendents: 300 were sent to prison for an average term of 13 years; 190 were public prostitutes; 680 were admitted alcoholics. His family, thus far, has cost the government more than $420,000. They made no contribution to society.

Jonathan Edwards lived at the same as Dukes. He loved the Lord and saw that his children were in church every Sunday, as he served the Lord to the best of his ability. He has had 929 descendents: 430 were ministers; 86 became university professors; 13 became university presidents; 75 authored books; 7 were elected to the United States Congress. His family never cost the government one cent but has contributed immeasurably to the life of plenty in this land.[11]

How grateful we should be for people who understand team leadership and turn away from autocracy except on occasions when it is necessary for a short time to elect that kind of behavior. To visit our continuum line once again before we close the chapter, it might be worth noticing that if one chooses a leadership style in the center of the line, it is not a great reach to move to free rein leadership or autocratic leadership when, on some occasion, either might be needed.

Parenting is a wonderful example of analyzing leadership behavior. When our children are young and immature, we lead them with a high degree of autocracy. Few three year olds have the final word in their meal-time or bedtime. As they become teenagers, however, we move to the middle of the line and try to cooperate in decisions regarding curfew and the use of

---

10. Ibid., 28.
11. Gangel and Bramer, *Genesis*, 312.

the family car. Finally, when they become adults and parents themselves, we wisely hold our tongues and let them make their own decisions regarding their life as a family and the way our grandchildren behave.

## 4

## Time to Turn Off "American Idol"

JUST BARELY into the twenty-first century the United States of America has given itself over to a culture of idolatry, not the worship of stones and wood, but the worship of people. Of course we have stumbled in this direction for decades—a culture both created and described by European art (Francis Schaeffer), then by the cinema around the world, and ultimately by television.

As I began this chapter it occurred to me to browse the prime-time programs for this week as shown in the newspaper television guide. Doubtless I missed more than half of them but in just a few minutes came up with *Dancing With the Stars, The Bachelor, Desperate Housewives, Heroes, America's Next Top Model, Biggest Loser, Deal or No Deal, ET, Survivor, The World Series*, the end of the NFL season, the beginning of the NBA season, and *Insider Edition*. No question about it, America worships its idols and delights when one of its favorite people becomes a superstar. Furthermore, that infatuation does not fade even when the star defames his or her own position as in the case of Howard Stern, O. J. Simpson. Michael Jackson or Paris Hilton.

Let me not give the impression that I claim part of this culture; I have never felt more alienated. It so happens that in Atlanta ABC delays its evening news so we can watch *NBC Nightly News* at 6:30 and then *ABC News* at 7:00. Immediately following both of those news programs, on two completely different networks, one encounters the show *ET* (*Entertainment Tonight*) blaring its chilling theme around the room before my arthritic fingers can grab for the remote and make a change.

Meanwhile, abortion, sexual promiscuity, crime, drug abuse, breakdown of the family, divorce, pornography, gambling, homosexuality and general civil disobedience all grow rampant. Our willingness to live with current trends in music, art, clothing and entertainment has taken us to lows our grandparents could not even have dreamt of. My Swiss grandfather became a believer late in life, but even before he trusted Christ just one verse of numerous contemporary rap songs would have driven him into a fury. J. Kirby Anderson states it in terms that cannot be misunderstood:

> The media often desensitize their viewers. Yesterday's sensation can become tomorrow's ho-hum. Television and film producers reach for bigger, better, more explicit scenes to build and keep audiences. Over time, viewers become desensitized to the sex and violence in the media. What was shocking ten years ago is generally accepted today.[1]

But this book does not target culture or contemporary mores. This chapter asks how we handle ministry situations in which our leaders have become international celebrities. As some wag once put it, "A celebrity is a person who is famous for being famous."

## Moses—Mighty Mentor of Israel

The writer of the "faith chapter" (Heb 11), under the control of the Holy Spirit, arranged the history of Israel according to its heroes of faith. Moses received a full seven verses compared to Abraham's twelve and one each for Isaac, Jacob, and Joseph. Samson, David, and Samuel barely merit mention, and Joshua doesn't even make the list though the walls of Jericho come down and Rahab briefly comes up.

Abraham founded the Israeli nation but Moses became its greatest hero. He appeared on the scene about 400 years after Joseph's time and you recall the story of his birth and rescue by Pharaoh's daughter during a crisis when all the first-born children of the Hebrews were killed. We could certainly list Joseph with the superstars but we have no record of anyone who worked with him or under his leadership. In a more regional sense, we could focus on Abraham (Hebrews 11) where national leadership lessons are scarce. But nowhere in Scripture do we see an up-and-coming leader trained and mentored by a superstar more clearly than the record of Joshua and Moses.

Moses' life unfolded in three 40 year periods: the adopted grandson of the Pharaoh; the exile to Midian, about 200 miles southeast of Egypt just north and east of the Gulf of Aqaba; and the Exodus and wandering. Old Testament scholars do not agree on the issue, but the popular theory claims that Moses spent his first 40 years under the powerful and cruel Rameses II, then returned to Egypt at the age of 80 to confront Merneptah. Some scholars believe that the princess who pulled Moses

---

1. Anderson, *Moral Dilemmas*, 198–99.

from the Nile was Hatshepsut, daughter of Thutmose, who lived some 200 years before Rameses II. If this third idea prevails, we know from history that Hatshepsut seized the throne after Thutmose II died, and ruled Egypt for 22 years.

Just to get our history straight, let's remember that Moses was born sometime between 1550 and 1500 BC; he led the Hebrews in the exodus from Egypt 40 years later and then from age 80 to 120 led them through the wilderness to the east bank of the Jordan. Slaves themselves, Moses' parents could hardly have imagined that he would be raised in the royal household. But surely Hatsheput's discovery and decision made headlines all over the empire. Nevertheless, we know of nothing that Moses achieved during the first 40 years of his life except the knee-jerk response of killing an Egyptian slave-master and hiding his body in the sand (Exodus 2:12).

Certainly Moses seemed more popular than Elvis by the time the ten plagues finished and Pharaoh literally chased his slaves east out of Egypt. They crossed the Red Sea leaving Pharaoh's army at the bottom and turned southeast toward Elim with Moses as their new "king." Add to that water from the rock, the Ten Commandments, the punishment at the golden calf, the building of the tabernacle and establishment of the priesthood. God granted him authority over some 2,000,000 people when Joshua finally enters the story as one of the twelve spies who entered Canaan from Kadesh Barnea (Num 13:2, 26).

After Caleb and Joshua brought courageous reports of trust in God, Joshua increased in authority and respect in the eyes of Moses and all the people. But I encounter no difficulty imagining this brave and strong young man often pondering when he would get a shot at becoming Head Shepherd, the CEO of Israel, the senior pastor of the congregation in the wilderness. As I write these words I cannot recall knowing any assistant pastor who waited 40 years for promotion to senior pastor in the same church.

Some argue that Joshua wrote this book himself, others hold out for a date as late as the 1200s BC. My own position surmises that most of the book was written by Joshua between 1406 and 1380 BC with some other portions added by editors or redactors at a later time. However, I wander from leadership to dabble in Old Testament history; we need not fight those battles here. Clearly in both the Pentateuch and the book of Joshua this man could not carry out his mission without the supernatural power God. But he would also fail if he could not win the support of the tribal leaders, "the officers of the people." Despite the great similarities between Moses and Joshua, we all agree Moses posed a tough act to follow.

Think also of the new leader who replaced the prophetic icon Elijah. Despite the striking similarities in their ministries and mannerisms, those two men led quite differently. Elijah unleashed spectacular miracles, national, and highly visible, whereas Elisha dealt more often with "little people" and common things such as water, oil, pottage, loaves, and axe heads.

The lesson seems simple—but so important. God calls His people to follow others who have served in the same capacity in earlier years. Too often we measure ourselves by the record of a predecessor, failing to realize that God does not expect us to match anyone else. Like Joshua, we must acknowledge the gifts and commands He has placed on us for our time. We can certainly learn from those who have gone before, but we don't want to fall into any of the traps or in any way restrict God's powerful hand by mimicking the ministry of another one of His servants.[2]

Clearly Moses does not fit the profile of toxic leaders we have discussed so far. Not because he didn't possess some of the qualities, but God imbued him with His own hands and voice. Since we always want to put the best light on the Bible, we find it easy to criticize these 2,000,000 people wandering around the wilderness with nothing but bread and water to eat without the slightest understanding of where they were headed. When the Israelites attacked the Midianites by order of God (Numbers 31) "They took all the plunder and spoils, including the people and animals, and brought the captives, spoils and plunder to Moses and Eleazar the priest and the Israelite assembly at their camp on the plains of Moab, by the Jordan across from Jericho" (vv. 11–12).

The text tells us that "Moses was angry with the officers of the army—the commanders of thousands and commanders of hundreds—who returned from the battle" and instructed those officers to "kill all the boys. And kill every woman who has slept with a man, but save for yourselves every girl who has never slept with a man" (vv. 17–18). Numerous incidents like this occur throughout the Pentateuch but the epitome of course, was the golden calf incident described in Exodus 32.

When they left Egypt the Israelites had taken anything they wanted, plundering jewelry and golden dishware from which they made ornamental parts of the Tabernacle—and the golden calf. In Exodus 32 we see God angry at the Israelites because He knows how they behaved while Moses went up on Mount Sinai. When Moses actually discovers this, his appeal for redemption from God's wrath changes considerably: "When Moses approached the camp and saw the calf and the dancing, his anger burned

---

2. Gangel and Bramer, *Genesis*, 8.

and he threw the tablets out of his hands, breaking them to pieces at the foot of the mountain. And he took the calf they had made and burned it in the fire; then he ground it to powder, scattered it on the water and made the Israelites drink it" (vv. 19–20).

Not exactly the same story as Jim Jones and the Kool-Aid, but nevertheless a brief glimpse at a fiery, sometimes impatient leader who grew disgusted with his people. At various times in his appearance throughout the first five books of the Old Testament Moses shows lack of wisdom, impatience, pride, anger, stubbornness and sometimes just a tinge of self or personal omniscience and omnipotence.

## Joshua, the Patient Assistant

Krista Henley warns us that "A toxic leader may bark out orders without respect for the receiver, or present unpredictable moods that keep employees afraid and vigilant. The red ink flows when time, productivity, and spirit are drained slowly out of individuals who encounter these top leadership and management styles."[3]

Let me say it again. Our loyalty to the heroes of the Bible becomes so great that we fail to see their shortcomings. When the people actually crossed the Jordan and entered the Promised Land, Joshua and Caleb were the only adults who might still have had bad memories of Moses' leadership and with their own great insight may have been able to understand his behavior on a variety of crucial occasions. But ordinary people were surely put off by many of the things Moses said and quite startled when he told them that if they were thirsty he, Moses, would get them water out of the rock. Imagine what they thought when Moses, having been told by God to "speak to that rock before your eyes and it will pour out its water," actually gathered the assembly and "took the staff from the Lord's presence and said, 'Listen, you rebels, must we bring you water out of this rock?'" (Numbers 20:6–11).

This sin that prohibited Moses from leading the people into the Promised Land occurred at the Waters of Meribah. I cannot call Moses a toxic leader, but I do see in his relationship with Joshua many of the problems that occur when second level leaders eagerly wait to take on greater responsibility while autocrats hold it even closer to their own hearts. In his article "Stopping Toxic Leaders" Vincent Ferguson says "These leaders have an uncanny knack for reading the climate of real and/or perceived needs and aspirations of individuals in their community; and they are well

---

3. Henley, "Detoxifying a Toxic Leader," 1.

able to articulate those needs. They project themselves as ready, willing and most able to satisfy them. In pursuit of their ambition, they create holy illusions of being genuinely concerned about personal and community development and empowerment, while all the while subtly maintaining support systems that disempower individuals and communities."[4]

Like it or not, that quote from Ferguson rather well describes Moses when his father-in-law Jethro visited him in Midian. Jethro watched as "The next day Moses took his seat to serve as judge for the people, and they stood around him from morning till evening. When his father-in-law saw all that Moses was doing for the people, he said, 'What is this you are doing for the people? Why do you alone sit as judge, while all these people stand around you from morning till evening?'" (Exod 18:13–15). Jethro goes on to offer a plan for reorganization that will pull Moses out of autocracy and help him depend more on other people. One of the greatest passages in the Bible on the leadership behavior of delegation appears at the end of Exodus 18: "Moses listened to his father-in-law and did everything he said. He chose capable men from all Israel and made them leaders of the people, officials over thousands, hundreds, fifties and tens. They served as judges for the people at all times. The difficult cases they brought to Moses, but the simple ones they decided themselves" (vv. 24–26).

## God, The Magnificent Controller of the Universe

If he had not been God's servant, Moses could well have been one of the worst tyrants in history. Only because the people knew when Moses spoke he spoke the truth of God could they put up with the inconvenience, delays, fits of anger and huge number of fatalities in the wilderness because of punishment.

I can almost hear someone say, "That's right. I'm a senior pastor and God speaks through me to the people and, like Moses, I occasionally indulge in pride, anger and stubbornness, but my people know that I stay close to the Lord and would not lead them astray." Sounds good except for one frightening flaw—Moses was the recipient of direct revelation; we form doctrine and behavior on the basis of our own interpretation. *There is a world of difference between having an infallible Bible and having an infallible interpretation of that Bible.*

Nevertheless, what arises in the pages of Scripture from the first chapter of Exodus to the first chapter of Joshua is a 120 year period in which God tapped one man to take all the public heat and lead the people

---

4. Ferguson, "Stopping Toxic leaders," 1.

during an escape and survival mode. Then he chose a very different man, the warrior who will take them into and through the Promised Land. Just think about what God said to Joshua in the first chapter of the book that bears his name. "Be strong and courageous. Do not be terrified; do not be discouraged, for the Lord your God will be with you wherever you go." (Joshua 1:9).

- Joshua could be confident because God is competent
- Joshua could be dependent because God is dependable
- Joshua could trust because God is trustworthy

When we stare at the Jordan River in our leadership lives, what do we see? The swirling muddy water of spiritual failures, sins, fears, and habits? Some persistent physical problem? The steady flow of broken relationships? Like Joshua, we need to take our eyes off the river and off our predecessors and fix them on the God of the river.

Traditionally we've thought of leadership as gifted people with special traits taking charge of the rest of us in order to make sure things get done. But the recent theme of leadership literature that centers on "the learning organization" and "team leadership" is much more in keeping with the biblical pattern, especially the New Testament. It centers on influencing everyone in the organization to achieve at a higher level. Let's close with the words of Bornstein and Smith:

> We submit that leadership in the future will more closely reflect a process whereby a leader pursues his or her vision by intentionally seeking to influence others in the conditions in which they work, allowing them to perform to their full potential and thus both increasing the probability of realizing the vision and maximizing the organizational and personal development of all parties involved.[5]

---

5. Bornstein and Smith, "The Leader Who Serves," 283.

# 5

# Incompetence Can Be Cured

NEARLY TWENTY years ago Warren Bennis' great book *Why Leaders Can't Lead* hit the marketplace and served as a late twentieth-century wake-up call. Chapters like "Learning Some Basic Truisms about Leadership," "The Long Slide from True Leadership," "Bosses As Heroes and Celebrities," and "When Losing Is Winning" became part of the new era in leadership studies, a revolution of thought regarding the leader's role in any organization. In the chapter "Dealing with the Way Things Are," Bennis reminds us that

> People in positions of authority must be alert, curious, impatient, brave, steadfast, truthful, and in focus; they must not only know what they see but say what they see. Gandhi said, "We must be the change we wish to see in the world." Thus, if people in authority believe that competence and conscience must be restored, then they must demonstrate both.

Earlier in the book he argues that

> Billions of dollars are spent annually by and on would-be leaders, yet we have no leaders, and though many corporations now offer leadership courses to their more promising employees, corporate America has lost its lead in the world market. In fact, to this point, more leaders have been made by accident, circumstances, and sheer will than have been made by all of the leadership courses.[1]

In research done for the book Bennis discovered what he calls four competencies evident to some extent in every leader: "Management of Attention; Management of Meaning; Management of Trust; and Management of Self."[2]

The leadership field has moved on to other emphases, but down-home garden variety incompetence continues to exact a demanding and depressing toll from employees in many lines of work. Competence simply

---

1. Bennis, 37.
2. Ibid., 19.

refers to a person's ability to adequately and satisfactorily complete the task for which he or she is responsible. The proclamation is always more important than the pastor; the mission always takes priority over the marketing; and achievement always supersedes acclaim. In *The Five Temptations of a CEO* Patrick Lencioni speaks about the most dangerous and most common failure in leadership.

> The most important principle that an executive must embrace is a desire to produce results. As obvious as this sounds, it is not universally practiced by the highest-ranking executives in many companies. Many CEOs put something ahead of results on their list of priorities, and it represents the most dangerous of all the temptations: the desire to protect the status of their careers.[3]

Let's be careful, however, not to push this crucial principle ahead of its balancing counterpart—*process*. When teaching week-long doctoral seminars in leadership I find myself saying multiple times a day, "Balance product and process." In fact, competence in both task management and people management form, in my opinion, the twin pillars of successful leadership. I agree with Hans Finzel when he says

> Many if not most Christian leaders in our country today tend toward being task-oriented. Even if it is not their nature or personality, it seems that the job of the modern-day executive leader demands it. We evaluate people by their accomplishments. Task-oriented people are the ones who get put in charge in the first place. They rise to the top of organizations by virtue of the large volume of tasks that they have been able to shove out the door. And the information revolution creates in an ever-growing pile of paperwork that the leader must somehow cope with and control.
>
> Some people tend to be *task-oriented* and some tend to be *people-oriented*. The problem arises because we have subtly made task-orientation more desirable in our leader selection process.[4]

This is hardly new thinking since Andrew Halpin analyzed such a strategic bi-modal analysis of every organization and introduced the adjective "transactional" to describe the hair trigger dynamic of this relationship.[5]

---

3. Lencioni, *The Five Temptations of a CEO*, 112.
4. Finzel, *The Top Ten Mistakes Leaders Make*, 43.
5. Halpin, *Theory and Research in Administration*.

# Lessons from an Old Man

Henry Ward Beecher once said, "The strength of a man consists in finding out the way God is going, and going that way." Once while playing in a golf tournament, Lee Trevino was hit by lightening out on the course. Shaken up but not seriously injured, Trevino was asked what he learned from the experience. He replied, "When God wants to play through, you'd better let him."

Well, God wants to play through. Not just to get in front of us, but literally to play through us in the game of leadership. Of all the attributes of God discussed in Scripture, holiness may be the most difficult to replicate in our own lives. But Peter could not be clearer when he says to all who read his first epistle, "But just as he who called you is holy, so be holy in all you do; for it is written: 'Be holy, because I have am holy'" (1 Peter 1:15–16). Peter quotes a variety of Old Testament texts in this epistle but puts this one right smack in a leadership passage because the next verse says, "Since you call on a Father who judges each man's work impartially, live your lives as strangers here in reverent fear." But what does all this have to do with incompetence?

The early chapters of 1 Samuel show us the darkest time in the history of Israel, between slavery in Egypt and captivity in Assyria and Babylon. In the late twelfth century BC, chaos and confusion ruled and the morale of the people fell into the very ground they walked on. The events of chapters 1–4 take place at Shiloh, about twenty miles north of Jerusalem, the location of the tabernacle during those ancient times. To understand the connection of Old Testament books we need to lift Ruth from between Judges and 1 Samuel and read Judges 21:25 as an introduction to 1 Samuel: "In those days Israel had no king; everyone did as he saw fit." We add to that 1 Samuel 3:1, which tells us, "In those days the word of the Lord was rare; there were not many visions." We sense the spiritual, cultural, and political doldrums into which Samuel was born.

But Samuel is not our spotlight character in this chapter—that dubious honor falls to Eli, the old priest presiding at Shiloh. Like us, he led in difficult days. And while the twelfth century BC seems light years away from our cyberspace culture in the twenty-first century, the task of Eli can be legitimately compared to the task of leaders today. Eli's failure in that role rises from the ashes of history to stare us in the face. Certainly Eli had no problem understanding God's holiness; the Bible never challenges the old priest's righteousness. But he could not reproduce the holiness which

God reflected in his life to his evil sons, Hophni and Phinehas. In short, as a father and as a priest Eli was incompetent.

## Competent Leaders Serve by God's Appointment

Eli had not usurped the priesthood in Israel; he was a legitimate high priest from the line of Ithamar, Aaron's youngest son. We all take pride in our work, our titles, our achievements, and the respect of our professional peers, but God's primary appointment for leaders centers on their homes not their jobs. Fathering is a vocation not a pastime, and because Eli proved an incompetent father he also proved an incompetent priest. Too many men fall into the traps sprung by failure at home that often drives them deep into job involvement where they feel more confident and successful.

Eli's story provides no solution, just a warning. God said to Eli, "I chose your father out of all the tribes of Israel to be my priest, to go up to my altar, to burn incense, and to wear an ephod in my presence" (1 Sam 2:28). God says to us, "I chose you to be a leader in your family and at your job, to serve as an example for your children and your employees, and I expect competence in both areas." You can't run from that appointment, and you can't hide from it.

W. A. Criswell, a famous Southern Baptist pastor now in heaven, tells about a time when as a seminary student he attended a Paderewski Concert in Louisville, Kentucky. The house was packed, but he found a seat in the front row, right next to a beautiful girl—a double win. They stood up to stretch when the house lights came on for intermission, so he turned to the young lady and said, "Isn't this the biggest congregation you've ever seen?" No, you can't hide it. And as Eli found out, you can't run away from it. God calls Christian leaders to lead in difficult days because they serve by God's appointment.

## Competent Leaders Put First Things First

One of my favorite school stories is about a third grader who walked up to his teacher's desk one morning to announce, "Miss Morgan, I don't want to frighten you but my daddy says if my grades don't improve, somebody is going to get a spanking." Perhaps, but not Miss Morgan.

In our contemporary culture, children enter schools with more secular baggage than ever before and the load gets bigger every week. Experiences come to them secondhand, rather like sitting in front of a television set watching a sunset scene while the actual sun sets outside. Then culture has taught them to value speed over reflection, graphics over argument, marketing over principle, hardware over interpersonal relationships and doing over being. Everything must be quicker, faster, farther, and sooner. But competence in leadership takes time and somehow in the harried, hassled world of leadership we leaders must demonstrate and communicate the process of seeking God and pass our search on both to our children and our employees.

As I said, you can't run from or hide from it—and you can't fake it. In the city of Joliet, Illinois, a pickup truck left a burglary scene and as a get-away maneuver stopped at St. John the Baptist Catholic Church. It happened to be during the service and the congregation was praying. The police had no problem locating the truck but, as they went into the sanctuary, they preferred not to disturb the worshippers by creating a fuss. So they simply walked up and down the aisles. No luck. None of the worshippers looked like a burglar. Finally, just before leaving, they decided to ask the priest, who mumbled a reply the officers could not understand. About that time they noticed he wasn't wearing a priestly collar and two suede cowboy boots protruded from under his long black robe. You can't fake it. Faking leaders become failing leaders. Incompetence strikes again.

We would all agree that fathers who neglect their children because they work 16 hours a day making millions to buy large estates and yachts do not glorify God, do not practice holiness, and invite God's judgment on their lives. We might be more lenient with a pastor or priest who spends as much time "in the Lord's work" that his own children choose the wide path to destruction. We might—but not God. He held Eli personally responsible for his incompetent handling of the godless behavior of Hophni and Phinehas and before this story ends, Eli is dead, both sons are dead, Israel has faced horrendous defeat by the Philistines, and the Ark of the Covenant captured. Just when you thought things couldn't get worse, that's exactly what happened.

## *Competent Leaders Hold God's Reputation in Their Hands*

God has little interest in our excuses, yet we seem to concoct them with ease. Have a look at this list of excuses actually written by parents to teachers to explain their child's absence from the classrooms:

- "My son is under the doctor's care and should not take physical education today—please execute him."
- "Please excuse my son's tardiness. I forgot to wake him up and I did not find him until I started making the beds."

- "Sally won't be in school a week from Friday; we have to attend a funeral."

Incompetent parents produce incompetent children and the fact that Eli was a priest cut him no slack with God.

To put it plainly, God holds leaders responsible for the general flavor and atmosphere of the organizations, departments or congregations they serve. A senior pastor supervising three or four assistants in specialty ministries certainly carries an "Eli-like" responsibility in dealing with those four people, men or women. His example as a thorough, humble, competent leader may well determine what those four people will become in leadership positions twenty years hence. Like our children, we often only have assistants and employees with us for a short period of time. After that, we may grieve, we may weep, we may pray about their failures, but our opportunities have past.

At this point it would be possible to think of the consequences of Eli's incompetence falling on Hophni and Phinehas, and certainly that happened. But we must also remember young Samuel growing up in an atmosphere which offered him no example of fatherhood and no example of godly leadership. You recall that when Hannah prayed in the tabernacle with her lips moving, Eli concluded that she must be drunk. Yes, Samuel became Eli's second chance and even though he served under an incompetent leader, he grew into one of the greatest leaders Israel ever had.

Eli's success with Samuel did not alleviate the inevitable judgment on him, his sons and his nation because of his prior failures, but it did leave Israel a godly priest and prophet. The lesson? Sincere, godly and willing young leaders can not only survive incompetent supervisors, they can thrive from negative lessons.

We could wish the story ended by the time Samuel anointed Saul as the first king. But the reason for that event demonstrates for us historically that Samuel reproduced his mentor's most tragic error. Apparently Eli taught Samuel well in matters of public worship and personal godliness, but he could not teach him how to raise godly sons. First Samuel 8:3 tells us about Samuel's family: "His sons did not walk in his ways. They turned aside after dishonest gain and accepted brides and perverted justice." The lives of Samuel, Hophni, and Phinehas overlapped for only a few years, but during those years Eli lived out both the risk and the opportunity of competent leadership.

## Thoughts on Becoming a Samuel

You won't find holiness on a shelf at the hardware store or in the halftime show at the football game; Christian leaders have to make their way through all the shallow thinking and downright heresy which surrounds us every day. When working for an incompetent supervisor we may have to exercise meekness and selectivity at the same time. To borrow a phrase from the New Testament, we need to be "wise as serpents and harmless as doves." What we hear and see must be filtered through the funnel of biblical godliness. On this we might take a tip from Dr. Seuss.

> My uncle ordered popovers
> From the restaurant's bill of fare.
> And, when they were served,
> He regarded them with a penetrating stare.
> Then he spoke great words of wisdom
> As he sat there on that chair:
> "To eat these things," said my uncle,
> You must exercise much care.
> You may swallow down what's solid but . . .
> You must spit out the air!"
> And as you partake of the world's bill of fare,
> That's darn good advice to follow.
> Do a lot of spitting out the hot air,
> And be careful what you swallow.

To the best of my knowledge that piece has never been published but was delivered by Dr. Seuss at a college commencement shortly before his death.

I held no leadership post whatsoever until my junior year in college. I had been a believer since the age of six but it never occurred to me that God might want to use someone like me to lead other people. I suffered from a spiritual problem of course, I had equated holiness with perfection—its biblical meaning had completely eluded me. Reading Tozer's *The Knowledge of the Holy* helped, but I didn't really get a handle on personal holiness until I worked my way through Lewis Sperry Chafer's *He That is Spiritual* and Francis Schaeffer's *True Spirituality*.

Leaders must value *relative* holiness with the full awareness that they will never achieve *absolute* holiness until they get to heaven. But in our lives, our families and our ministries we want to raise the bar as high as possible. Competence means getting rid of those lame excuses and holding ourselves, our families, our colleagues, and those whom we lead to the excellent standards of God. That doesn't happen overnight, of course. Sanctification involves becoming more like God and therefore more able to help reproduce His character in our people.

In an article entitled "Leadership Development Needs of the Business World" Blair Sheppard and Joe Leboeuf argue that the standards of leadership are rapidly rising. "Competence must be coupled with a level of leadership heretofore unseen, anchored by a solid commitment to integrity and ethics."[6] I commend these contemporary leadership specialists, these authors who stress ethics and integrity, naming the pharmaceutical and oil industries as examples of corporations which have not accepted these essentials. Sheppard also echoes the constant cry in the literature for developing a culture of leadership:

> Given these challenges, perhaps the most critical requirement of leaders today is to create a culture that builds leaders. We cannot know the challenges those who will lead in the future will be confronting. We can predict that their choices will be harder and that the requirement for leadership will percolate lower within organizations, especially as the speed and complexity of business operation continues to increase.[7]

Perhaps of greatest value in this article is the authors' identification of "Three Leadership Tasks." Effective leaders:

- Preserve the integrity of their organizations
- Create an umbrella of protection for others
- Create conditions for the effective development of other leaders[8]

---

6. Sheppard and Leboeuf, *Leadership Development Needs of the Business World*, 7.
7. Ibid., 11.
8. Ibid., 12.

# 6

# Ignorance Is Definitely Not Bliss!

Pastor Petroff had served at Family Community Church for 12 years during which time he had seen the membership quadruple—from 40 to 160. As a part of the twelfth anniversary celebration, FCC announced that they had been secretly building a fund for a second full-time staff member and had accumulated a full year's salary. They invited Pastor Petroff to determine the kind of help he needed and, with the assistance of an ad hoc personnel task group, to hire another full-time person. He was beside himself with joy. He had wisely kept his nose out of church finances, never complained about having too much work and too small a staff (FCC employed a 20-hour-a-week secretary/receptionist), and took great joy in his people's maturity to understand the growing needs of the church.

Since many of the newer members were young parents, Pastor Petroff and the task force decided to create the position of "Pastor to Families" and put that person in charge of children and youth ministries. Within six months Pastor Alex, 29, a mature seminary graduate with two small children, came to FCC to begin his first full-time ministry.

So far the story is almost idyllic and we would expect nothing but huge success from the combined efforts of these two leaders. But we only know that Pastor Petroff is patient and wise, two wonderful characteristics for a pastor. We don't know if he has any experience in children's ministry or youth ministry, if he has ever supervised anyone (the secretary has a clear picture of what he expected of her and "takes care" of things in the outer office without supervision), or if he plans any preparation to change his own life and leadership style at the arrival of Pastor Alex.

But you are still wondering why I use the adjective "ignorant" in this chapter. Because ignorant does not mean stupid, witless or unschooled. It simply means having insufficient knowledge of a specific area to deal with it satisfactorily. For example, I am nearly totally ignorant with respect to how an automobile works and how to repair anything under the hood. I am also ignorant regarding any aspect of plumbing other than pouring liquid Draino down the hole of the sink or tub. This great void comes from having no father at home and never living in a house we owned until after I was married. I have transferred most of this ignorance to my son who also has an earned doctorate and whom no one would think of as stupid or slow. Once we capture the true denotation of the word, we can see the ignorant gap in Pastor Petroff's life.

How does that make him a toxic leader? Because the popularity of his new Pastor to Families, the enthusiasm and eagerness with which he was welcomed, and the immediate church growth which followed, somehow drove the two men apart. Unable to get comfortable with his new role of supervisor, Petroff withdrew into a monastic, jealous separation that prevented any possibility of pastoral team relationship, much less the perpetuation of the team concept throughout all the lay leaders. Marsha Whicker says that toxic leaders "have a deep-seated but well-disguised sense of personal inadequacy, selfish values and cleverness at concealing deceit."[1]

I'll end the story by telling you that Alex stayed just about two years, left for another position with great hesitancy and sadness and FCC plunged into a protracted period of stagnancy though Petroff stayed on for another ten years. Please understand that Pastor Petroff did not intend any of this. *Toxic leaders are not usually deliberately toxic, nor do they always recognize their own toxicity.*

## Two Different Men

Elijah and Elisha were two of the most colorful and interesting prophets of Old Testament times. Elijah began his ministry when Jehoshaphat (873–848 BC) reigned in the southern kingdom and Ahab (874–853 BC) in the north. After Ahab, Elijah dealt with Ahaziah and after Jehoshaphat, with Jehoram. He took on the prophets of Baal (1 Kings 18). He also worked with Jehu, Jehoahaz, and Joash, the latter two the most godly in the list. Elisha on the other hand is famous for the Prophets Seminary, a school of the prophets described in 2 Kings 4. He is also famous for the unique "prophet's chamber" developed by a prominent couple in the town of Shunam. He raised the Shunammite boy from the dead, healed Naaman of leprosy, and coped with the Syrian threat.

All of this happened in the ninth century BC while these two men ministered in the northern kingdom of Israel and to a lesser extent, the southern kingdom of Judah. At the command of God Elijah threw his mantle on Elisha, thereby anointing him to be the next leader and spokes-

---

1. Whicker, "When Organizations Go Bad," 2.

man for God. For a time Elisha served as his assistant but we catch no glimpse of mentoring or teaching from this fiery, self-contained servant of God, likely at least a full generation older than his successor. To be sure, Elisha behaved almost as strangely as Elijah but he seems to have poked around in an effort to find his own way rather than relying on the careful preparation his discipler could have given him.

We want to be careful here because the Bible itself does not criticize Elijah for the way he handled the transition. But if we compare that experience with Paul and any of his protégés (Luke, Titus, Timothy, Epaphras) or with Barnabas and John Mark we see a completely different approach. I like to refer to it as the *new covenant model of leadership versus the old covenant model of leadership*. Obviously, a monarchial culture such as that in which both Elijah and Elisha lived is much less sensitive to team leadership and cooperation than the early church where we see multiple examples of people ministering together, beginning with the seven servants of Acts 6.

## Learning to Supervise Effectively

Why couldn't Petroff have sincerely thanked God for the arrival of Alex and asked for wisdom to mold and train the younger man for whatever God had planned for him in the future? Why did he feel threatened and isolated? Why did he allow Satan to put little seeds of jealousy in his heart so that he couldn't accept or affirm the ministerial accomplishments of his assistant? Because as a toxic leader, he did not know how to combat these evil tendencies that come to all of us in leadership roles. In fact, Petroff was ignorant because while it competently pounded Greek, Hebrew, Systematic Theology, and Historical Theology into his head, his seminary never required a single course in leadership during his entire three year MDiv program.

I cannot tell you how often I have seen this play out from both sides of the picture. For the past twenty years I have been teaching leadership at the doctoral level in nearly a dozen seminaries. I have talked to 40- and 50-year-old pastors who felt caught in "the Petroff trap" and 25 and 35 year-old assistants who, when I told the skeleton of the Alex story, thought I surely must know about their personal situations. I have prayed with pastors, wept with them, scolded them, recommended major changes in their leadership styles, and a huge percentage of all that effort centered on supervising or being supervised.

Quality supervision, exactly like leadership itself, is learned behavior. Some people may have a great tendency toward patience, clarity of com-

*Ignorance Is Definitely Not Bliss!*

munication and willingness to give up segments of their control. But all of this forms standard leadership behavior and can be learned just as one learns to start a fast-break in basketball, defend against a screen play in football or keep a runner on second base while still playing adequate shortstop in baseball. If you don't believe this, go to some country where they have only known soccer and try to teach them how to play tennis.

We have several family phenomena in the National Football League as I write—twins Tikki and Ronde Barber playing for Tampa Bay and the New York Giants; and even more highly visible, the Manning brothers Peyton and Eli, sons of former Minnesota Vikings quarterback Archie Manning. Peyton is a super bowl all star and Eli shows great promise. Why? Because they have Archie's genes? Obviously they do. But I'm very confident that Archie's thousands of hours of coaching contained much more value.

## So What Do I Do? Quit?

Sometimes that becomes necessary as the only solution, but I never recommend it as the first choice. In fact, in my opinion, it is always the last choice. In an article entitled "The Wrong Stuff" posted on www.fastcompany.com, Margaret Heffernan talks about surviving toxic bosses in her particular business culture. She suggests five specific steps Alex might have taken to keep him at FCC and perhaps build bridges from his side of the river rather than waiting for Pastor Petroff to do so, though we all recognize Petroff should have taken the initiative.

- Recognize what is happening. Alex has to be sufficiently mature to understand that the ignorance at play in this situation is not of his making. He needs to be confident in God's call and understand that his own training reflected a considerably modified seminary curriculum from two decades earlier.

- Tell someone so you can hear yourself describe how you feel. This excellent idea almost always helps and sometimes a spouse represents the best choice—sometimes not. In a case like the one Alex faced, a spouse would probably be discouraged and derailed even before the victim and therefore unable to get a handle on the dilemma. But virtually every ministry type has a professional organization through which Alex could have contacted others of his own age, profession, and facing some of the same problems.

- Try to figure out whether you exist in a toxic culture or just work for a toxic boss. Heffernan does not refer to the national culture, as frighteningly toxic as we find the first decade of the twenty-first century. She's talking rather about the organizational culture, in my illustration, the culture of FCC which, from what we know about it, could not be called toxic. Indeed, we have already observed that Pastor Petroff does not fit the typical toxic profile; he has simply allowed the fault of ignorance to blind his handling of his first staff member.

- Keep a copy of any bullying emails, notes and letters. This good suggestion does not necessarily apply to Alex's case. What he might do, however, is keep a copy of every unanswered email or phone call since his senior pastor's neglect began.

- Tell friends and family so you can get support. Here again we must be careful. If Alex's friends and family attend FCC, he should not discuss his ministry problems with them. If, however, they live in another state many miles away, this suggestion will work.[2]

None of this speaks to the role of the church board in this situation. In a church of 160+ members, a breakdown in relationship between the senior pastor and his only associate could never go unnoticed. The lay leadership at FCC could hardly step in and fire Pastor Petroff after they had just honored him for a successful and satisfactory 12 year period of ministry. Yet, lay leaders will often have better training in leadership and supervision than pastors and their involvement on an authoritative basis of intervention might well have saved this ministry marriage.

This chapter exemplifies a phrase Peter Senge used for the title of an article not long ago—"Missing the Boat on Leadership." Senge is a senior lecturer at the Massachusetts Institute of Technology and the founding chairperson of the Society for Organizational Learning. He writes,

> The quality of our leadership depends on the quality of our awareness. Our awareness often suggests a world of obstacles and adversaries. It presents a reality of people and problems separate from ourselves. Such awareness shapes our goals in ways that limit our creative potential. . . . Not only do negative visions prevent us from focusing on what we want to create, they also subtly re-enforce a point of view that "we did not create these problems, somebody else did." This attitude of victimization robs us of our sense of con-

---

2. Heffernan, "The Wrong Stuff," 3.

nectedness to a large world, then, regardless of our success, leaves us feeling smaller rather than larger.[3]

---

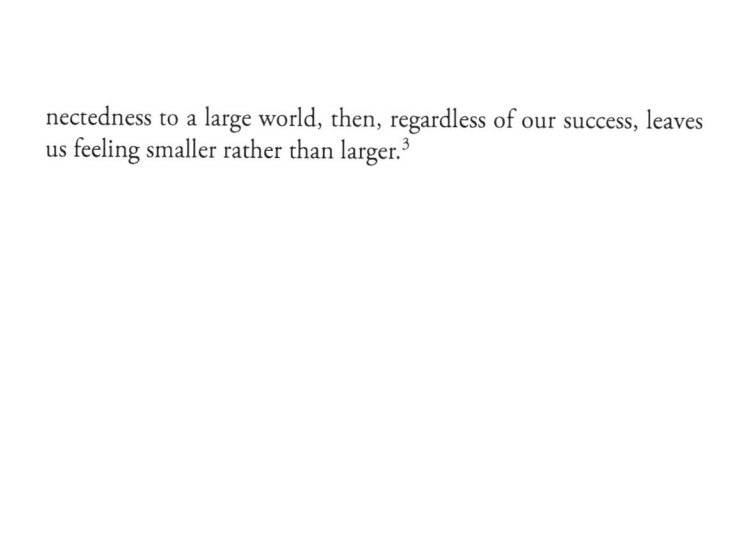

3. Senge, "Missing the Boat on Leadership," 29.

# 7

# Cruel Leaders Are the Worst

T. D. Jakes, author of *Maximize the Moment* (2000), also released *The Ten Commandments of Working in a Hostile Environment*, published by Berkley Press in 2005. Jakes writes from his clergy and media climate, summarizing his approach to vocations by drawing on the stories of the Bible as well as liturgical quotes and prayers. He makes much of the concept of vocation, imploring his readers to remember that God has reasons for people to stay on or leave jobs. The book articulates Ten Commandments of getting along in a hostile environment and lists the benefits of looking at work through positive and spiritual lenses. For example, Jakes tells his readers, "Do not expect to be appreciated."[1] He argues that if one makes appreciation a goal, one can easily fall into the pit of pandering to pleasing people rather than serving God and fulfilling one's vocation.

This useful advice fades into cliché when one arises each morning to face a cruel leader for another day. Of all the forms of toxicity, this one is surely hardest for any of us to handle. Yet every reputable leadership expert today emphasizes that the way we treat people is enormously more important than what we pay them or how lavishly we furnish their work areas. One could go so far as to say that cruel leadership reflects the very inverse of biblical team leadership. In one of the most important leadership books written yet in this century Jim Collins explores his research on how leaders go from "good to great."[2] Assuming you serve a good church, what would it have to do to become a great church? In his research Collins learned that moving from good to great does not require high profile leadership or celebrity personalities. Indeed, the kind of leaders who take churches, colleges, and seminaries from good to great tend to combine extreme personal humility with intense professional will and even shun celebrity and constant visibility. I'm assuming here you have not made the error of equating good to great and "large to larger."

---

1. Jakes, *The Ten Commandments of Working in a Hostile Environment*, 37.
2. Collins, *Good to Great*.

Furthermore, Collins' team discovered that one cannot achieve great things without great people. The staff we build around us from the president to the rookie combine their efforts to take an organization from good to great from the inside out. In such a task we would expect to find complexity and expense but Collins argues for *simplicity* and *personal passion*. He claims that if you have the right people on the bus, the problem of how to motivate and manage people largely goes away. But if you have the wrong people, it doesn't matter whether you discover the right direction—you still won't have a great organization. Collins tells us "When in doubt, don't hire—keep looking."[3] The minute you feel the need to tightly manage someone because of possible blunders that could embarrass the mission, you know you have made a hiring mistake. Collins does not mince words: "Letting the wrong people hang around is unfair to all the right people, who often find themselves compensating for the wrong people's inadequacies."[4]

That should be enough to whet your appetite to read the book, and also enough to support the idea that Christian organizations have no room for cruel people, much less cruel leaders.

## How Can a Christian Leader Be Cruel?

Cruelty arises most primitively not from the past experiences of the toxic leader as it does from just plain sin. Invariably it reaches and consumes our relationship with subordinates and destroys the organization. In other words, a toxic leader spreads the toxin until other people who have no history of cruelty feel forced to emulate such behavior at some level and eventually poison the entire organization until it dies. It's just a guess, but I would estimate that at least 50% of all Christian leaders fail miserably in connecting with subordinates. Some simply cannot grasp how people in their own organizations feel (a Christian college president selected from the business community or the pastorate). Others have never learned to control their emotions (an angry pastor who bullies the deacons or church members). And some just do not know their own people (the mission executive of a large board out of touch with issues and problems in the trenches).

None of these people intend cruelty; they have let down their defenses to the possibility of such behavior. In all the words that Lipman-Blumen chooses to describe "toxic behaviors" or "toxic qualities" (stifling destruc-

3. Ibid., 114.
4. Ibid., 126.

tive criticism, misleading followers, promoting incompetence, lack of integrity, insatiable ambition, enormous ego, arrogance, amorality, avarice, cowardice, and failure), the word *cruelty* never appears. Nor does it appear in the index. In her chapter "Leadership in Crisis: the Dangers of Creating God," however, she does talk about rising authoritarianism in crises.

> For current leaders who cannot cope, crisis may undo them. For other sitting leaders, particularly those who are foundering, crisis can help them establish a new agenda, find their direction, and renew their "creditability." Crisis also sets the stage for the emergence of new leaders, charismatic and other would-be heroic leaders, posing radical solutions. Crisis also makes us vulnerable to toxic leaders, who use such occasions to introduce authoritarianism.[5]

## Maintaining Dignity in the Face of Cruelty

A distinguished man in history understood leadership, administration, and cruelty and balanced all of them in a foreign nation in a most outstanding way. His name was Daniel. On the subject of leadership, the New Testament teaches didactically while the Old Testament offers more models. And among the many examples of good leadership we find, two stand out—Nehemiah and Daniel. I would guess that many thousand more Americans know the name and location of Babylon than did five year ago. The name goes all the way back to the Tower of Babel (Gen 11), and we find brief mention of "a beautiful robe from Babylonia" in Joshua 7:21. But not until the major prophets does Babylon catapult to its prominence in the Old Testament record. The written history of the city begins about 2800 BC, describing a significantly advanced civilization in the Mesopotamian valley. Sargon the Magnificent stretched the Babylonian kingdom from Persia to the Mediterranean Sea between 2360 and 2180 BC.

Then came the Elimites and after them the Amorites and the period scholars called "Old Babylonia" (1830–1550 BC), which included the reign of the famous Hammurabi (1726–1686 BC). Discovered on an eight-foot-high column of black diorite at Susa, the code of Hammurabi contained 282 paragraphs on criminal law. From this amazing document scholars learned a great deal about Babylonian civilization and the Akkadian language.

---

5. Lipman-Bluemen, *Toxic Leadership*, 108.

For the next eleven hundred years dynasties came and went until Tiglath-Pileser, became king of Babylon in 729 BC. This famous king who figured so prominently in the virgin prophecies of Isaiah 7 was conquered by the Assyrian Sennacherib in 689 BC and Babylon went once again into a tail-spin.

The Neo-Babylonian Empire began with Nabopolassar, who took charge in 625 BC. His victories over Nineveh and the great Pharaoh-Necho of Egypt built the kingdom that he handed over to his son Nebuchadnezzar.

Nebuchadnezzar's conquest of Palestine actually took place in three phases. The first, described at the beginning of chapter 1, occurred in 605 BC; the second in 597 BC; and the third and final one in 587 BC. The captivity lasted seventy years until the first exiles returned to the land, led by Zerubbabel. Sir Robert Anderson once wrote about the text of Daniel "By the test of chronology, therefore—the severest test which can be applied to historical statement—the absolute accuracy of these Scriptures is established."[6]

Much of the information at this point in our chapter derives directly from my commentary on *Daniel* published by Broadman and Holman in 2001 and available for those readers who want to follow the record of that book more thoroughly. Here I can suffice it to say that both Nebuchadnezzar and Belshazzar were among the most cruel and wicked kings in a very cruel and wicked era of history. Before three chapters have finished Daniel has told us about two different kinds of punishment put forth by Nebuchadnezzar. In chapter 2 the Chaldean faculty was threatened with having their bodies "cut into pieces" and their "houses turned into piles of rubble." There seems to be little evidence that this represented a standard form of execution in Ancient Babylon and might well have been some hideous instant whim of the king or one of his lackeys.

A short time later Daniel's three friends faced a "blazing furnace." In chapter 5, while the forces of the united Medes and Persians surrounded the territory of Babylon having already conquered the suburbs, Belshazzar threw a gigantic orgy including wild revelry and specific blasphemy. We would be wrong to think this an act of carelessness or mere stupidity. Certainly Belshazzar was both, but the record in Daniel seems to portray a distinct contrast between the gods being worshipped at the feast (Babylonians had no secular feasts) and the use of the sacred temple objects of the living God to celebrate and worship false gods. Pagan revelry had

---

6. Anderson, *Daniel and the Critics Den*, 22.

become brazen idolatry and defiance of the God whom Nebuchadnezzar had called "the King of heaven" (4:37).

In his fresh paraphrase, *The Message,* Eugene Peterson describes Belshazzar and all cruel leaders from the words of Jeremiah.

> "The city wall of Babylon—those massive walls—
> Will be flattened.
> And those city gates—huge gates!—
> Will be set on fire.
> The harder you work at this empty life,
> The less you are.
> Nothing comes of ambition like this
> But ashes." (Jer 51:57–58)[7]

## Surviving a Cruel Leader

Before we conclude that modern civilization no longer puts people in situations such as those Daniel faced with such grace and dignity, let me remind you that in multiple countries of the world right now people are starving, homeless, held in slavery, constantly persecuted, imprisoned, and murdered by twenty-first century rulers. No, the world no longer fears Saddam Hussein, but the world worries about North Korea's Kim Jung Il, the 5'3" dictator with a bouffant hair style and elevator shoes. *Newsweek* writes, "History is not just about abstract forces like economics or ideology or geography. It is also shaped, often most divisively, by the aims and ambitions of deeply flawed men—men like Kim, his father and generations of North Korean soldiers, scientists, and spies who have spent years trying to join the Nuclear Club."[8] Jung's development of his present nuclear arsenal ravaged a generation of scientists sent like worker bees into toxic nuclear labs. It cost billions in hard currency that might have fed starving people, and hobbled the national economy by imposing perpetual austerity.

Daniel not only survived Belshazzar's orgy but also the pit of lions designed by Darius and the conquest of Babylon by the Persians. The prophecies of Daniel leave us in awe and much less than full agreement on their meaning. But the behavior of this man as a leader contains no fuzziness or confusion. The righteousness of God rubbed off on His prophet. Daniel stands in stark contrast to many Pharisees of the New Testament, particularly the one in Luke 18 who "prayed about himself." Few Bible

---

7. Peterson, *The Message,* 7.
8. Hirsh, Michael, Melinda Liu and George Wehrfritz, 31.

prayers pinpoint empathy with other people and the humility and brokenness we see in the prayer of Daniel's ninth chapter. Self righteousness forms one of the great sins of religious people even though the Bible condemns it repeatedly. Every abused person, struggling in the tentacles of a cruel leader should hold firmly to Luke 18:14: "For everyone who exalts himself will be humbled, and he who humbles himself will be exalted."

Psalm 118 stands in a very interesting position in Scripture. I do not mean to suggest that God has placed it there for any special reason, but certainly its message anchors the ship of our theology. Psalm 117 is the shortest chapter in the Bible and Psalm 119 the longest. The Bible has 594 chapters before Psalm 118 and 594 chapters after Psalm 118. Within the psalm itself, one could say that verse 8 is the middle verse of the entire Bible and it proclaims the axiom, "It is better to take refuge in the Lord than to trust in man."

That's the way Daniel lived. That's the way he survived cruel leadership. That's the way he handled a toxic culture. He had every reason to abandon his faith in the God of Israel when the kingdom of Judah was taken captive to a foreign land. But God constantly strengthened him through dreams and visions, and Daniel never wavered in his faith.

Every Christian's relationship in the church as the bride of Christ finds expression in Scripture from the Gospels to Revelation. When John the Baptist heard that his disciples were defecting to Jesus, he said, "The bride belongs to the bridegroom. The friend who attends the bridegroom waits and listens for him, and is full of joy when he hears the bridegroom's voice . . . he must become greater; I must become less" (Jn 3:29–30).

I can imagine Daniel and John having a discussion in heaven in which John expresses his appreciation for Daniel's wonderful model of service to cruel leaders as well as his book of prophecies. Daniel responds by commending John for his role in the early days of the New Covenant people and wanting to know what it was like to be taught personally by Jesus for three and a half years.

# 8

# Bully for You!

In 2006, *Harvard Business Review* carried an article by Roderick M. Kramer entitled, "The Great Intimidators." One finds it difficult (having watched even a single episode of "Seinfeld") to take an article by someone named Kramer seriously. Furthermore, the article affords the most unbalanced and startling piece of journalism the HBR has published in a decade. In writing my leadership literature newsletter (*THE SEAL*), I attempt to select articles which promote concepts and techniques of leadership with which I agree and which I feel need more exposure and emphasis. I judiciously avoid utilizing an article or a book just for the sake of pointing out its faults, but Kramer pushed me over the edge. He exalts leaders with "bold, political intelligence" who "are not averse to causing a raucous, nor are they above using a few public whippings and ceremonial hangings to get attention. . . . These leaders seem to relish the chaos they create because, in their minds, it's constructive. Time is short, the stakes are high, and the measures required are draconian."[1]

Kramer makes a special point of distinguishing between "social intelligence" and "political intelligence." "While leaders with social intelligence use empathy and soft power to build bridges, politically intelligent leaders use intimidation and hard power to exploit the anxieties and vulnerabilities they detect."[2] They make millions for the adoring stock holders and take home their own millions only to finally bail out on a golden parachute of stock options after firing 20,000 people. Jesus once called them "the kings of the Gentiles" and said to His disciples, "You are not to be like that."

But how do Kramer's great intimidators behave? As one might expect, "The devil is in the details and the details can be found in the effective—but sometimes extreme—tactics these leaders use to coerce their subordinates to over-perform."[3] Direct confrontation is a favorite tactic of the

---

1. Kramer, "The Great Intimidators," 90.
2. Ibid., 91.
3. Ibid., 92.

50

*Bully for You!*

great intimidator. He or she will invade your space and do it as publicly as possible. Anger and rage play an important part in "political intelligence." Kramer finds this attractive because "people will think twice before confronting you if you have a reputation for being willing to scorch a little earth rather than back down."[4]

To Kramer's credit he throws in one page on "Managing Great Intimidators," suggesting that one can get such a person to want to mentor him by "doing your homework, working harder, laughing at their antics and earning their respect, calling their bluff, keeping your perspective and sticking around."[5] Perhaps. And for some people, there may be no option. As for me, I'm with Tevya's rabbi: "Rabbi, is there a prayer for the Czar?" "Oh, yes my son. 'May God bless and keep the Czar—far away from us!'"

That a major voice from the business world could speak through one of the three top business magazines on a subject like this the way Kramer handles it less than two years after the publication of *The Allure of Toxic Leaders* contributes to the impression that Kramer wants to run to the rescue of the Hitlers of the world and the church, defending the worst possible leadership behavior.

In an earlier chapter I mentioned that Lipman-Blumen does not use the word *cruel* at any strategic point in her book, though she constantly talks about cruel leaders. Neither does she mention the word *sin*, which we would not expect since she writes below the theological radar.

What kind of legacy do cruel leaders leave? Kouzes and Posner have been dealing with this problem since their first book in 1985, but *A Leader's Legacy* published in 2006 returns to the subject.

> We have said this many times, and it's worth repeating again. *Leadership is a relationship between those who aspire to lead and those who choose to follow* (italics theirs). There may have been a time when leaders could command commitment, but those times are long passed. People follow people, not positions. If there is not some sense of personal relationship, then it's just less likely that people will want to follow.[6]

---

4. Ibid., 94.
5. Ibid., 93.
6. Kouzes and Posner, *A Leader's Legacy*, 52.

## Ahab—A Kramer Favorite

One intimidator's historical background embodies evil, bullying, sin and all the other characteristics of the great intimidators. The kingdom of Israel, divided into north and south in 931 BC, shook like a young tree in a tornado 57 years later when a fellow by the name of Ahab began to rule the Northern Kingdom (we spoke of him in an earlier chapter in connection with Elijah). He reigned 22 years during which sin and idolatry went unchecked in Israel. Beers says,

> Ahab's greatest mistake was his marriage to Jezebel, a wicked woman who worshipped Baal and tried to force this god on the rest of the Israelites. King Ahab was not strong enough to subdue his wife's evil habits, and soon found himself following her sinful practices. Ahab was a strong military leader and a great builder, but he rarely listened to God. He finally died in battle against the Syrians in 859 BC.[7]

The Old Testament contains numerous additional incidents in which Ahab brings to full bloom the behavioral traits of a toxic leader. Full of himself and empty of God, proud of his buildings and his battles, he was snatched into death in the great battle at Quarqar fighting against Shalmaneser III, the Assyrian. Ahab's son Ahaziah took the throne in 853 BC.

### *How Modern Day Ahabs Fight and Function.*

For her primary illustration of leadership brutality, Lipman-Blumen selects Al Dunlap who followed Roger Schipke at Sunbeam. Her source is John Byrne's book *Chain Saw: The Notorious Career of Al Dunlap in the Era of Prophets-at-Any-Price.*

> Their new boss [Dunlap] sat at the table like an imperial demagogue. He cheered his own past accomplishments, reminding the men that he had done eight turnarounds on three continents and Sunbeam would be his ninth. He even urged them to buy his forthcoming book, Mean Business: How I Saved Bad Companies and Made Good Companies Great, so they would know exactly what he expected from them. . . . "It was like a dog barking at you for hours," Boynton later said. "He just yelled, ranted, and raved. He was condescending, belligerent, and disrespectful." According to Attorney Fannin "It was a very, very hostile environment. Everything was a confrontation and a put-down.[8]

---

7. Beers, 244.
8. Lipman-Blumen, 206.

Bullying hardly offers a strong enough term for this kind of behavior in a leader. Like Ahab, Dunlap was downright evil, a public exhibition of deliberate sin—and it happens thousands of times a year in churches all around the world. We see multiple sins here—anger, pride, greed, and many more.

But leaders do not always bully through shouting and cursing, they can do it simply through quiet lies like Enron chairman Ken Lay. We were stunned to learn that

> . . . even when Enron employees found the retirement accounts in shambles as the company's stock plummeted, they committed to support their leaders. Many kept purchasing stock on the advice of Chairman Lay, who urged them to buy (and to recommend the stock to their friends and relatives) at the once-in-a-lifetime bargain price, which, Lay insisted, was bound to go up.[9]

Since Lay is no longer with us, we will never know whether he deliberately lied or just functioned in hopeless incompetence, both symptoms of toxicity.

We'll wait until chapter 12 to discuss in detail specific measures we can take to defeat, neutralize or escape toxic leaders, especially bullies. But here I want to explore just a bit further the chaos these people create wherever they go, especially in ministry situations.

## Counting the Costs

Recently a great article in *American Way* entitled "Monster Managers" claimed that 42% of U.S. workers reported incidents of yelling and verbal abuse in their workplaces and 30% admitted to yelling at their co-workers themselves! In other words, rather than refusing toxicity because they see its destructive qualities, workers in an organization begin to replicate the toxic behavior from above like poison ivy spreading from the hands to the hips to the knees to the feet.

One website listed six common characteristics filed by 2,000 people that would most likely make them "walk out the door."

- Belittles people: ranks number one with both men and women
- Lies: ranks number two with both men and women
- Micromanaging: ranks number three with men

9 Ibid., 206

- Condescending or demeaning: ranks number three with women and number four with men
- Humiliating or embarrassing others: ranks number five with men and number four with women
- Acts arrogantly: ranks number five with women[10]

One of the common myths about leadership in this country is that heroes will always arise who stand above the pack ethically and morally and we crave their example. Certainly that can happen, but history teaches us that tendency toward sin creates the natural order and honest, ethical even humble behavior in ministry is only possible through the power of the Holy Spirit in the lives of leaders.

## When Power Corrupts

I graduated from seminary and began full-time ministry in the year John F. Kennedy was elected President of the United States. Everyone loved him with his beautiful wife, model children and masculine good looks. Later we all found out that he had a countless number of mistresses, a poor relationship with his wife, and something akin to contempt for his staff. Lipman-Blumen picks this up in an incident described by Richard Reeves in his intriguing book *President Kennedy: Profile of Power*.

> "You see Kenny there," he said once as O'Donnell slept on a plane. "If I woke him up and asked him to jump out of this plane for me, he'd do it. You don't find that kind of loyalty easily." Of Mrs. Lincoln, his secretary, the President said that if he called to inform her that he had just cut off Jackie's head and wanted to get rid of it, the devoted secretary would appear immediately with a hat box of appropriate size. Need I explore this issue further? Franklin D. Roosevelt pulled more tricks behind the scenes than we will ever know in dividing up the world after World War II, to say nothing of the Constitutional violation that gave him an unprecedented third term. Richard M. Nixon was often pictured praying with Billy Graham in the Oval Office but Billy was horribly embarrassed when the tapes came out and the President's vituperative anger filled books. How the Democrats loved their young governor from Arkansas and his brilliant wife who had reenergized the party in 1992; and how they stood back in anger and shame when

---

10. Margaret Heffernen, "The Wrong Stuff," 2.

he was impeached by the House of Representatives, though the verdict was not upheld in the Senate.[11]

## *Toxic Saints*

Lipmen-Blumen reminds us early in her book,

> Even exemplary leaders have some toxic chinks. Some exemplary not-for-profit leaders have stepped over the line in their zeal to reach their allotted goals. Political leaders too, some among the most admired—such as Franklin D. Roosevelt, Harry S. Truman, and even Abraham Lincoln—occasionally have acted in ways that we would be hard pressed not to label "toxic."[12]

Even the saints are not completely "toxic free." According to Christopher Hitchens, Mother Teresa blithely accepted a donation from financier Charles Keating, of the Savings and Loan scandal. Subsequently, the founder of the Order of the Missionaries of Charity wrote to presiding Judge Lance Ito, attempting to intercede on Keating's behalf in the sentencing phase of his trial. So let's be realists and remember that even beloved icons of leadership can display human frailties.[13]

## *Four Dangers*

When we read the paragraphs above we wonder if we ourselves, even though we might at present be the victims of toxic leadership behavior, could someday become toxic either as followers or leaders. Right after 9/11 when Rudolph Giuliani walked around New York with the aura of a god for his magnificent bravery and spectacular leadership during that catastrophe, he seriously entertained replaying the Roosevelt routine and allowing his people at City Hall to set aside the law to make him available for a third term as mayor. At the last moment he changed course and still remains a respected national figure. We want to follow leaders like that, but in doing so we might very well set ourselves up for a fall. Four warnings seem useful as we draw this chapter to a close.

- *We dare not give personal responsibility for our own futures to the hands of our leaders.* America has been called "a nation of sheep" who desperately desire leaders and will follow those who seem strong

---

11. Ibid., 157.
12. Lipman-Blumen, *The Allure of Toxic Leaders*, 152.
13. Ibid., 6.

and capable of achieving what they want. But God has made us individuals, small groups and families and we dare not let powerful personalities, especially toxic leaders, take away that right. Esau did it once and his descendents still regret that stupidity.

- *We dare not forget the reality of sin.* In speaking to the corporate business world Lipman-Blumen's book dared not wander into the realm of theology. But I'm speaking to the ministry world and every Christian ought to be reflecting a question asked decades ago by one of the most brilliant psychiatrists in America—"Whatever happened to sin?," the title of a book written by Dr. Karl Menninger to emphasize the complete irresponsibility into which our society has fallen. My friend Bob Pyne writes,

  > In every case sin is portrayed as a violation of the ideal. It injures proper relationships or is described negatively as lawlessness, disobedience, impiety, lovelessness, unbelief, distress, unrighteousness, unthankfulness, wrongdoing, or faithlessness. It is a fall from a right standing, and unnatural descent into darkness from light. As Daniel Doriani wrote, "Sin opposes God's law and His created beings. Sin hates rather than loves, it doubts or contradicts rather than trusts and affirms, it harms and abuses rather than helps and respects." Its purposes are determined negatively in opposition to the will of God, prompting Berkouwer to write, "Evil has no thesis in itself but only antithesis." It is contra, always against what is good.[14]

- *As present or future leaders we also place ourselves in jeopardy for abuse and remorse if we unthinkingly put our lives and services at the disposal of toxic leaders*, encourage their activities in any way, refuse to stand up to them, or by our own desperate need, actually create them.

- *We also place ourselves at risk by allowing even temporary authoritarian or autocratic leadership.* As I said in an earlier chapter, at times autocratic leadership is not only legitimate but necessary. However, we had better understand clearly the risk we take when saying something like, "Pastor, we're delighted you're here. We support you in everything and know you'll lead us in the right path."

---

14. Pyne, *Humanity & Sin.* 207, 208

Thinking Christians understand that dominant autocratic leaders who bully and threaten to retain power, may stand a mere step away from cruelty, but miles away from the cross.

# 9

# "It's My Way or the Highway"

THIS CHAPTER spins directly off the last because it reminds us that good leaders can have toxic traits and that future leaders form their own toxicity even as you read these words. We can see a close link between the demanding leader and the bullying leader with whom we closed the last chapter, though a much longer path winds between the beginning demand and the behavior of bullying.

Demand often occurs during crisis situations in which we desperately need someone to take over the organization and either rescue it financially or provide new vision (I will say more about *vision* later). Lipman-Blumen puts it this way:

> Crises often cry out for tough measures. Faced with falling profits, corporate bosses demand curtailed travel, as well as hiring, promotion, and salary freezes. In severe crises, such as wartime, a leader's call for curfews and rationing may be both necessary and appropriate.

And again,

> It is not surprising, then, that we actively seek the embrace of strong, even dictatorial leaders. Set adrift in threatening and unfamiliar seas, most of us willingly surrender our freedom to any authoritarian captain.[1]

The Homeland Security Act, subject of great debate and division of opinion, has reminded many of Benjamin Franklin's somewhat scornful observation (which I paraphrase here), "They who give up essential liberty to obtain temporary safety deserve neither liberty nor safety." Indeed, a great revolutionary pep talk one-liner. On the other hand, a government that cannot guarantee the security of its citizens (Lebanon, for example) cannot offer those citizens freedom. Perhaps the best quote in history to provoke proper awareness when dealing with a demanding leader is the great paragraph delivered by Martin Niemoeler.

---

1. Lipman-Blumen, *The Allure of Toxic Leaders*, 99, 100.

When Hitler attacked the Jews I was not a Jew, therefore I was not concerned. And when Hitler attacked the Catholics, I was not a Catholic, and therefore, I was not concerned. And when Hitler attacked the unions and the industrialists, I was not a member of the unions and I was not concerned. Then Hitler attacked me and the Protestant church—and there was nobody left to be concerned.[2]

## Struggles of a Spiritual Son

Placing Timothy in the shadow of Paul and suggesting that the great apostle of the New Testament might have shown some toxic characteristics strikes me as the hermeneutical equivalent of attacking apple pie and motherhood. Nevertheless, few would disagree with the idea that Paul often functioned as a demanding leader. To heighten the impact of the text, I draw once again from *The Message*.

> It's obvious, isn't it, that the law code isn't primarily for people who live responsibly, but for the irresponsible, who defy all authority, riding roughshod over God, life, sex, truth, whatever! They are contemptuous of this great Message I have been put in charge of by this great God (1 Tim 1:10–11).
>
> I don't let women take over and tell the men what to do. They should study to be quiet and obedient along with everyone else (1 Tim 2:11, 12).
>
> Servants in the church are to be committed to their spouses, attentive to their own children, and diligent in looking after their own affairs (1 Tim 3:12).
>
> Exercise daily in God—no spiritual flabbiness, please! Workouts in the gymnasium are useful, but a disciplined life in God is far more so, making you fit both today and forever (1 Tim 4:8).
>
> Any Christian woman who has widows in her family is responsible for them. They shouldn't be dumped on the church. The church has its hands full already with widows who need help (1 Tim 5:16).
>
> Tell those rich in this world's wealth to quit being so full of themselves and so obsessed with money, which is here today and gone tomorrow. Tell them to go after God, who piles on all the riches we could ever manage—to do good, to be rich in helping others, to be extravagantly generous (1 Tim 6:9).[3]

---

2. Neimoller, *Congressional Record*, Oct. 14, 1968, 31636.
3. Peterson, *The Message*. 432–439.

And those all appear in just the first epistle to Timothy! Your response might be, "But all those things are true and good." Exactly. One could argue that by his demands Paul rescued Timothy from toxicity. I only intend to point out that Paul did demand with some regularity and we know demanding leaders stand just one notch away from autocracy on that continuum line we looked at in chapter 3.

## Unseen Intruders

Just in case you didn't read the author's introduction, let me say again that all the stories in this book represent true experiences of real people whom I know. However, names, locations, and other details have been changed to protect both the innocent and the guilty. So consider these two very different anecdotes from my personal leadership experience.

### *The Talented Candidate*

A large mid-western congregation learned that it would soon lose its popular and charismatic senior pastor to the presidency of a para-church organization. He announced his departure a year in advance, a transition team of elders, lay people and staff was formed, and a list of candidates drawn up. From that list and at the departing pastor's suggestion, one young man seemed to emerge. An outstanding biblical scholar, he could explain the Bible clearly and authoritatively and no one considered his preaching boring. One problem consistently nagged the transition committee—he had never served as a pastor before at any level.

In my view, this would have automatically removed him from the list, but the church pushed on. After several visits they grew comfortable with him and named him to succeed the retiring pastor with still six months before his departure. Since he was already "hired," and the appointment announced, the church gave him a credit card to be billed to its financial committee and even the doubters decided to make the very best of the situation.

Then staff members began to get long-distance calls from the newly appointed pastor suggesting massive reorganization, re-titling, and other changes the candidate would institute upon his arrival. In fact, he wanted the staff to start these revisions immediately. Meanwhile the financial committee received credit card billings for materials that had no seeming relevance for a person who would not even arrive for another six months.

Sometimes in a church the nervous branches rattle out in the pews; this time it began with the staff. Within a month after the appointment three out of four associate pastors turned in written resignations to the senior pastor, who courageously tried to hold everything together for a few months before leaving. When news of their resignations blended with the cries of the finance committee, the huge error became obvious. The congregation could have gone ahead with the plan, but it would have found itself a completely different church. In short, the board withdrew the invitation and the search continued.

That church had dodged a bullet. The congregation would have been in ruins; the staff, an effective working group under their present leader, would have been off in every direction. The departing pastor would know that he had a voice in recommending a situation that could do nothing but harm his flock. And the candidate, though quite blithely ignorant of the issues, radiated toxicity before he ever sat behind the desk or stood behind the pulpit. Actually, my metaphor lacks punch. The church did not dodge a bullet; it avoided a huge explosion.

### *The Suspicious Resume*

One of the great faith mission boards with a record of 75 years of service to the body of Christ sought a new leader. A search committee, consisting largely of the trustees but including a few missionaries as well, began the search. The field missionaries did something the board had never seen before. They polled all active missionaries serving with that board asking their opinions regarding the qualities they wished to see in their new leader and a document of several pages emerged. Early in the search committee discussions, the members reviewed this document. Pronouncing it well done, the search committee accepted it, while making no promises to fulfill what the missionaries felt they needed.

After months of effort, the search committee could not and would not bring a single name before the Board of Trustees. In fact they not only presented three names and resumes without recommendation or bias, but had those candidates available for interviews—all on the same day!

Each candidate spent about an hour with the board of trustees followed by a goodly amount of discussion. The second candidate, though lacking the qualifications and experience in the portfolios of both numbers one and three, was a fast-talking, promise-the-world-and-more type of person who simply ignited several key trustees with his passionate claim, "God has called me to lead this mission." After vociferous politicking by the candidate's backers, the chairman told the board they would have two votes. If the first affirmed a majority, the second would proclaim unanimity. In a matter of minutes, assuming any discussion had now been put behind them, the board voted 16 to 9 to call candidate number two and someone immediately said, "I move to make it unanimous," and they did.

Within a few months the mission's new chief executive officer took his place and began, not unlike our pastoral candidate in the story above, to rearrange the deck chairs all facing the captain's cabin. The mission faced a number of genuine challenges at that point and the new CEO promised they would be met and met soon. A "wait and see" attitude prevailed as the mission slowly plunged deeper into debt.

All of sudden a missionary-in-training, someone unknown to any of the trustees, sent a letter to the Chairman of the Board indicating that the new executive director did not have a Doctor of Ministry degree from a major seminary as his resume had declared. The director countered by arguing that such a minor inconsistency could only be due to a secretarial error because he had taken a number of classes at that institution. Unable to determine whether the erroneous resume indicated a simple mistake or deliberate deceit, the trustees made one more effort to hold on to their appointee—they asked the entire missionary force for a vote of confidence in their new leader. He lost. He left. And the progress of that mission stuttered, delayed by a year of looking, two years of learning, followed by another year of looking.

## Leadership Lessons from Church and Mission

Toxicity flows all through both these stories and I have watched some of the people involved weep as they explained to me what happened. But let's just quickly look at the foolish decisions along the way to see how toxicity spread its ugly tentacles through these two normal and healthy Christian organizations.

1. In both cases the organizations showed willingness to settle for people who had neither the qualifications nor the experience to do the jobs available. In fact, they had written sound and useful profiles of the kind of leaders they needed and then reversed themselves, ignoring the profiles in their selection.

2. Since some of the businessmen in the church recognized what we now call "toxic leadership," they were able to cancel that package before it arrived. Unity returned well before the new pastor took over and all the assistants stayed.

3. Confirming the details in the resume should have been a routine part of the work of the Search Committee. Regardless of whether

the candidate faked the degree or simply made a simple mistake, it should have been amply discussed by the Search Committee before the board ever received the nomination.

4. The idea of giving a new pastor a credit card from the church six months before he arrives defies all reason. Yes, he asked for it, but that alone should have been a tip off that a toxic leader would soon lurk among them.

5. The idea of "making something unanimous" exemplifies a leadership fallacy that many organizations and denominations still clasp to their collective breasts. The intent seeks to avoid telling the new leader that a certain percentage of his superior officers (the board) had opposed his election. But the majority who favored the appointment cannot trample over the rights of the minority and force them to say something else. Every time I have watched this practice in action it frightens me again that people can blindly imagine everyone believing that the entire board of trustees actually approved the chosen candidate. I'm told that in the crucial mission board meeting, one trustee stood up at the end and angrily challenged the rest, "If any word of this vote gets out, you'll have to answer to me!"

Since we have been playing around a bit in Paul's first letter to Timothy let's close this chapter with that wonderful paragraph describing the requirements for elders.

> If anyone wants to provide leadership in the church, good! But there are preconditions: A leader must be well-thought-of, committed to his wife, cool and collected, accessible, and hospitable. He must know what he's talking about, not be overly fond of wine, not pushy but gentle, not thin-skinned, not money-hungry. He must handle his own affairs well, attentive to his own children and having their respect. For if someone is unable to handle his own affairs, how can he take care of God's church? He must not be a new believer, lest the position go to his head and the Devil trip him up. Outsiders must think well of him, or else the Devil will figure out a way to lure him into his trap (1 Tim 3:1–7).

# 10

# Sinking the Sloth

One would think this chapter should come at us from the opposite perspective—eager leaders suffering the sloth of lazy employees. And no doubt in the church that happens with much greater frequency than we care to admit. Others might challenge this chapter on the basis that laziness in a leader seems hardly as toxic as bullying or deception. But in the broadest sense, *anything that corrupts the positive ongoing of a ministry organization deserves the label "toxic behavior."*

## How Laziness Corrupts Leaders

When one thinks about it, one certainly recognizes that almost any form of effective ministry depends to a great extent upon *personal initiative* and the *control of discretionary time*. In this sense, a lazy person who becomes a pastor or an elder might very well provide a toxic barrier to the enthusiastic service of other staff members, other church officers, and the congregation as a whole. Toxicity does not have to involve ranting and raving; it simply describes a poisoning of the atmosphere in some way. In fact, the toxicity of laziness can surface in a ministry organization much more quickly than in a profit-making industry where "the bottom line" will sooner rather than later display the failures of sloth exactly where it occurs. Nor should we group laziness with incompetence. The incompetent leader simply does not know what to do; the lazy leader knows what to do but refuses to do it.

Hari Shetty, a principal consultant at Wipro, offers

> . . . . two factors that would cure a leader from becoming toxic: a) an organizational structure that is transparent and people movement is encouraged. Good employees would never want to work for a toxic leader thereby reducing chances of success for the lazy leader. And b) formal feedback mechanism for reportees and peers about performance of leaders with respect to their job descriptions.[1]

---

1. Shetty, *Leadership: How to Spot a Toxic Boss*, 3.

As we shall see in our final two chapters, some responsibility for the creation and endurance of toxic leaders must rest with their followers. Daniel Liechty tells us

> Those who eagerly push [lazy people] into leadership positions, in business, education, religion, politics, and many other areas of life, almost surely release the potential toxicity within them. It is the responsibility of followers to help them keep this in check, to create reasonable boundaries, and also strongly act as a check to emerging toxicity, and also to nurture toward positions of leadership responsibility among those not so eager to lead. A healthier future will depend on this.[2]

The toxicity of laziness often surfaces in families. Eager wives scramble to meet the family budget because lazy husbands don't work hard enough; husbands who work long and hard watch their income drained by a spend-thrift wife who can't resist the use of credit cards; parents wring their hands over lazy children who want to live life surrounded by food, television, ipods, Sirius and the latest video games. Toxic laziness also has a biblical foundation in the short New Testament book of Titus.

## Leading Slothful Servants

Consider Titus, an uncircumcised Gentile Christian who visited Jerusalem with Paul after the third missionary journey (Gal 2:1–3). His name does not appear in Acts but shows up 13 times in the rest of the New Testament. After ministering in Corinth, Titus went to Crete, told to stay there as Paul's representative. He later carried out a mission to what is now modern Yugoslavia, and we read of him the final time in 2 Timothy 4:10.

Apparently, the young man found his experience at Crete most difficult, and there he proved his leadership ability. Crete is the fourth largest island in the Mediterranean, lying directly south of the Aegean Sea. In the first century its inhabitants had slipped into deep godlessness with three particular sins targeted—dishonesty, gluttony and laziness. In his letter to Titus which we have as part of our New Testament, likely written between AD 63 and 65, Paul admits that he understands the problems there.

> For there are many rebellious people, mere talkers and deceivers, especially those of the circumcision group. They must be silenced, because they are ruining whole households by teaching things they ought not to teach—and that for the sake of dishonest gain. Even

2. Liechty, http://staff.washington.edu/nelgee/hidden/hidn_5.htm, 2.

one of their own prophets has said, "Cretans are always liars, evil brutes, lazy gluttons." This testimony is true. Therefore, rebuke them sharply, so that they will be sound in the faith and will pay no attention to Jewish myths or to the commands of those who reject the truth (Titus 1:10–14).

Paul takes his quotation from Epimenides, a sixth-century BC Cretan. Let's notice here the Apostle does not accuse Titus of laziness but rather the people he must deal with, quite possibly some of the major lay leaders of the church on that island.

The Bible hardly confines the sin of sloth to Titus' struggle with the Cretans. Clear back in the book of Proverbs we read,

> I went past the field of the sluggard, past the vineyard of the man who lacks judgment; thorns had come up everywhere, the ground was covered with weeds, and the stone wall was in ruins. I applied by heart to what I observed and learned a lesson from what I saw: A little sleep, a little slumber, a little folding of the hands to rest—and poverty will come on you like a bandit and scarcity like an armed man (Prov 24:30–34).

Sloth violates one's family, one's community and one's church. Jesus spoke of a slave who buried his talents in the ground (Matt 24:14–30). We too often handle laziness (sloth) as a bad habit that one can correct if he or she merely decides to do so. However Henry Fairlie claims that sloth is "a state of dejection that gives rise to torpor of mind and feeling and spirit; to a sluggishness or . . . a poisoning of the will; to despair, faintheartedness, and even desirelessness, a lack of real desire for anything, even for what is good."[3]

## *The Lazy Layman*

Jerry Logan accepted the pastorate at Suburban Bible Church after ten years of difficult but profitable work in church-planting. Planting churches often becomes something of a burn-out vocation and his denomination seemed quite happy to give him a break and let him work in a normal and apparently healthy congregation. The transition went well and Jerry served at SBC well over a year before he discovered that his five elders behaved a bit like statues in a museum; they looked real, even to the smallest detail, but they never moved.

Checking the constitution and by-laws, Jerry discovered the document clearly defined duties for the elders and included such ministries as

---

3. Fairlie, *The Seven Deadly Sins Today*, 113.

assisting the pastor in church discipline, counseling, visitation, and general spiritual oversight of the church. When he raised this point in an elder meeting, no one objected. In fact, no one said anything and no one did anything. They had settled into a pattern under their previous pastor who micro-managed the church by working fourteen hour days and taking responsibility for everything.

But they had fallen (almost without noticing it, and certainly not intentionally) into a functionless apathy. Once again, let me clearly state that I would rather have five quiet, apathetic elders than five screaming, raving, angry elders. In fact, I think I would rather have five slothful elders than one caught up in the toxicity of anger and out of control.

But that does not release us from the Bible's condemnation of laziness as sin. Nor does it solve the long-range problem, already visible at SBC, in which the laziness of the elders slips like a fog over the rest of the congregation and dampens it into ministerial paralysis.

## *Waking the Elders*

James C. Hunter and Associates have developed the leadership philosophy that forms the foundation of companies like Southwest Airlines, Starbucks and ServiceMaster. Early in his book *The World's Most Powerful Principle*, Hunter defines leadership as "the skill of influencing people to enthusiastically work toward goals identified as being for the common good, with character that inspires confidence."[4] His book hammers on principles I have drummed into hundreds of students over the past half century: Leadership is not management, and not about being boss, leadership is an awesome responsibility, a skill, and influence. And leadership is about character. Every reader should immediately see that a lazy leader violates every one of those principles.

Hunter carefully defines the difference between power and authority. "Power is the ability to force or coerce others to do your will, even if they would choose not to, because of your position or your might. Whereas authority is the skill . . . of getting others *willingly* to do your will because of your personal influence."[5] He points out that while one can buy and sell power, authority is never subject to such whims. Pastor Logan could greatly profit from Hunter's entire book but particularly from chapter 8 in which the author describes how one implements the development of character. Hunter touches on emotional intelligence and offers a map which

---

4. Hunter, James, *The World's Most Powerful Principle*, 53.
5. Ibid., 53.

can lead us to insure long-term behavioral change. The ingredients include "foundation (set the standard); feedback (identify the gaps); and fraction (eliminate gaps and measure results)."[6]

Now that Logan has discovered the deficiency in his elders he dare not conclude that somehow he can bring about a magical change by the sheer motivation they will imbibe from his own work ethic, spiritual life, and biblical preaching. Certainly all of those things will help and SBC will profit from each of them. But genuine motivation is not an external aura or cape thrown over another leader by the chief. It is unlocking what Hunter calls "a fire within people."[7]

## Turning Laziness into Leadership

For SBC to move out of stasis and into orbit will take more than an aggressive young pastor with ten years experience in church planting. It will take a level of competence and confidence from those five elders which arise from a conscious sense of accountability, collaboration, and inspiration. Such behavior will give people around them the ability to withstand difficult circumstances and setbacks. Confidence bridges expectations and performance as well as investments and results. It serves as a balance between arrogance and despair, and arises out of a history of how the church has functioned in the past.

Jerry's self-confidence will build confidence in the elders through supportive team-oriented behavior. Then SBC can begin to exercise confidence in itself, to reinforce its accountability and innovation. Finally, that will spread to people outside the church who will get on board because they naturally gravitate toward confidence shown by people who know their lives have been changed and who believe in the power of God in their congregation.

Any other options? I give Jerry about five years to produce the results I just described. If that does not happen, Suburban Bible Church probably faces rapid leader turnover which cannot set the stage for winning cycles or effectiveness. Rapid turnover always sparks losing streaks, escalates cycles of decline, and erodes confidence in the church. Rosabeth Moss Kanter talks about "learned hopelessness," surrendering to the timidity of mediocrity. Such leaders trap themselves in "doom loops" so that poor responses to problems actually exacerbate the problems. What follows in an organization whose leaders have become lazy? According to Kanter, SBC had better brace itself for nine marks of a losing organization:

6. Ibid., 173–76.
7. Ibid., 187.

- Decreased communication
- Rampant criticism and blame
- Eroded respect
- Increasing isolation
- Focus turning inward
- Turf guarding and small cliques
- Paralyzed initiative
- Dying aspirations
- Contagious negativity [8]

Avoiding these will not provide a secret formula for effective leadership. Nor should anyone equate confidence with arrogance nor substitute it for the control and power of the Holy Spirit. But the elder board needs to learn that sloth carries with it a subtle form of arrogance that causes them to *reject their accountability*. *They must work hard at collaborating* with ministry teams, *understand how to support other leaders* throughout the church and *communicate the kind of information* that will keep present ministries vibrant and strike fire under new ministry opportunities.

---

8. Kanter, *Confidence*, 136–38.

# 11

## Entering the Detox Lab

In November of 2006 the Associated Press interviewed actor Russell Crowe who had pleaded guilty the previous year to third-degree assault for throwing a phone at a hotel clerk. According to the reporter Crowe responded by saying, "Where I come from, a confrontation like that, as basic and simple as that, would have been satisfied with a hand shake and an apology." He said almost exactly the same thing on "60 Minutes" a few days later. Crowe shows no remorse whatsoever nor does he sense any guilt in this kind of public anger. "You've got to have a temper," he told the reporter, apparently considering this phase of his personality a necessary evil in living the life of a superstar. Perhaps he has had too much gladiatorial training.

This chapter asks a very difficult question: "Am I the problem?" If a high level of toxicity hangs in the air at your work place; if other employees quit and you can't quite understand why; if you find yourself leaving the building each day with bitterness or malicious thoughts about other people—you may be the problem. *Never forget that toxic leaders rarely recognize themselves.* Here's Lipman-Blumen again.

> Toxic leaders, particularly as they slip deeper into paranoia and toxicity, frequently devote the lion's share of their energies to controlling their followers (despite the evidence that followers often control themselves). Encouraged by the lack of restraint from the outside, much of their attention is devoted to developing new, more grandiose projects, courting the media, and imposing increased measures of repression. These measures include the shaping of new policies and structures to keep the followers from unseating the toxic leader.[1]

---

1. Lipman-Bluemen, *The Allure of Toxic Leaders*, 186.

## Discovering Your Own Toxicity

You don't need some kind of psychological test to see if you are a toxic leader, just review the characteristics we have discussed in this book and see how many apply to you. If you have any question, put them on a list and have the people you lead check the ones they think pertain to you. Bacal puts it as plainly as one could:

> For every toxic organization, there is a toxic leader, a leader who, by virtue of his or her own problems, creates an environment that drives people crazy. Toxic leaders are much like poor parents in that they exhibit certain behavior patterns that confuse and paralyze others who depend on them. . . . In short, the toxic manager confuses subordinates, uses very subtle ways of punishment for real or imagine transgressions, creates a high degree of dependence and is internally conflicted.[2]

How does one enter his or her own homemade detox lab without creating a big fuss? Actually, once you admit you have the disease, you are well on your way to the cure. Doctors treat toxins with antitoxin. As I mentioned in chapter 1, if you are bitten by a poisonous snake, some medical person will stick a needle in your arm and pump you full of specific antitoxins to deal with the poison of that particular snake. So the first room in the detox lab helps you identify not only that you carry toxicity but that certain aspects of your leadership may poison your organization, most likely something you never intended. For example, let's assume you are neither unethical nor amoral, reasonably credible, extremely competent, and even visionary. But people withdraw from you because of momentary lapses of control and restraint which make you appear seriously angry and unable to control your temper. You sound exactly like my friend Andrew.

Andrew, or Andy as we call him, appeared to all his employees "a strong leader." However, leadership experts today rarely use that terminology because for decades it went hand-in-hand with an authoritarian spirit that sought to control other people. How does one control other people? Possibly by threats, often by a reminder of the leader's authority and power in the organization, but perhaps most commonly by anger. Some people may fear your anger while others just find it extremely distasteful. The point is, they have no idea when it will break out so they walk around on edge every time you're near. I'm offering the easiest route to change. Most experts on leadership toxicity argue that you must have help from outside.

---

2. Bacal, "Welcome to The Fire of an Unhealthy Workplace," 3.

Krista Henley states it rather firmly in an article entitled "Detoxifying a Toxic Leader."

> When a difficult leader or manager is wreaking havoc, sending him or her to a course on leadership will do nothing to alter the behavior that stems from deep-seeded negative belief systems, blind spots, and unconscious behavior. Team building, in the traditional sense, will not elevate the pain of those around the bully. Style inventories, or other courses that highlight differences, will not change the situation. All of these methods aim at the intellect and neglect the more basic human components and the uniqueness of every individual. . . . We build walls of resistance around soft spots from such injuries, and thus we create holes in our soft skills abilities. Those holes cannot be filled by fancy quotes or leadership jargon. The core issues must be addressed head on, and with ongoing regular feedback that insures that goals are attained and that the negative behavior is eliminated. Soft skills change is slow in development. It is important to be aware of the short course, quick fix programs, which are also expensive, and do not yield positive results with toxic leaders.[3]

Which brings me right back to Andy. He is a bit older than I, but we have had similar experiences in Christian leadership down through the years and have known each other for over three decades. It wasn't until we both worked for the same organization that I noticed this fault in his character. Basically, he loves people and would not deliberately injure anyone's personal psyche or bring discouragement. But he has no idea what his temper outbursts produce in the lives of his staff. I watched him get frustrated one day because he couldn't find a certain person he needed. He burst into a conference room in which I was chairing a meeting and virtually shouted, "I'm looking for Harold! Where is he?" I replied in my softest, most gentle voice, "I'm sorry Andy, he is not here and none of us knows where you might find him at the moment." Without another word he left the room.

I've often wondered whether I should have gone to him personally and raised that point. Truthfully, I did not do so because I agree with Henley—the advice of a friend would likely fail to derail that life-time habit. Make no mistake about it, bursts of anger do not belong only to toxic leaders, they provide temptation to all leaders.

---

3. Henley, "Detoxifying a Toxic Leader," 2.

*Entering the Detox Lab*

## Monarchial Toxicity

Few Bible characters can claim the kind of toxic behavior we see in Israel's first king—Saul. In Saul's defense, we should note that he did not want the job in the first place but because of Samuel's corrupt sons, God condescended to giving His people a king. At first Saul behaved humbly and even seemed shy about his appointment. But by 1 Samuel 13 we find him deliberately disobeying God and offering a sacrifice, intended only for Samuel. Saul was born of the tribe of Benjamin and lived in the city of Gibeah which became the headquarters of his military campaigns. He spent his life battering and being battered by the Philistines whose government consisted of five rulers and a highly organized army of skilled warriors.

Since at that time only the Philistines knew the secret of making iron, the Israelites found themselves at great disadvantage in battle. When Saul most desperately needed him, David came along and immediately became the king's favorite. But his exploits and the laud of the people echoed too often in ears of the greedy, jealous king who actually became demented, only soothed by David's playing of a lyre, an instrument similar to a small hand harp. After one particular victory against the Philistines, Saul and David marched back into the city at the head of the army and the women sang that provocative song, "Saul has killed his thousands, but David his ten thousands." From that point on David laid low until Saul met his death on the slopes of Mount Gilboa, about sixty miles north of Jerusalem.

Beers tells us, "It is little wonder that Saul fell on his sword and killed himself when faced with the prospect of being captured by the Philistines, enemies who hated the Israelites. As a prisoner of war, and especially as a captured king and commander in chief, Saul would have been humiliated before all the Philistines and brutally tortured."[4]

In his early days Saul did reasonably well under the mentoring of Samuel, an older, more experienced authority figure who could talk to the king in plain Hebrew. After Samuel's death, Saul tried to manage his goblins by himself and failed miserably. The angry, jealous king ended up with his body fastened to the walls of a town named Beth Shan.

## Leader, Heal Thyself

None of this, not even the biblical story of Saul, gives us a definitive Christian picture of what one can do if one considers oneself a toxic leader.

---

4. Beers, *The Victor Handbook of Bible Knowledge*, 204.

The following suggestions I have seen work in people who determine to carry out a self-detoxification program:

1. *Publicly admit any behavior which has caused your people hurt or discouragement.* This is exactly what I did the second month into my first college presidency. Hired as a change agent to rescue a rapidly failing institution, I went in, sleeves rolled up, chin set to the task, eyes straight ahead and made the changes. By the end of the first month the faculty and staff felt as though they worked for an automaton who certainly had the competence for his leadership task but didn't care anything about people. When my assistant told me that, it broke my heart. I felt no anger at them for fearing me; I was disappointed at myself for not immediately developing a team-centered servant leadership approach. That was a long time ago, and I never made that mistake again; but it took the rest of that first year to straighten it out.

2. *Ask for forgiveness and prayer and make someone you trust a monitor of your public behavior* so you can learn immediately if you are falling into the trap again.

3. *Be patient.* Even after recognizing your toxic failure, it can take ten months to restore a confidence you lost in ten days. It's not just you that must change, but you must also dismantle a system that allowed you to be a toxic leader in the first place. I think Danah Zohar puts it well:

> If we want to change systems, we have to change human behavior. But human behavior is not so easily changed. To achieve real transformation, we have to change the motivations that drive behavior. That is the prime responsibility of a visionary leader. Today business, politics, education, and society in general are driven by four negative motivations: fear, greed, anger and self-assertion. When we are controlled by these negative emotions, we both trust ourselves and others less, and we tend to act from a small place inside ourselves.[5]

We began this chapter with Lipman-Blumen and we can close it the same way. She talks about "opportunities to learn how to resist and organize resistance" and says

---

5. Zohar, "Spiritually Intelligent Leadership," 50.

Grasping that you know how to take the high ground, as well as guarding and nurturing your own talents, can build your self esteem and give you the leadership edge. Gandhi eschewed weapons of violence. He relied primarily on taking the moral high ground, which ultimately defeated his heavily armed military opponents.[6]

---

6. Lipman-Blumen, *The Allure of Toxic Leaders*, 196.

# 12

## Terminating Toxicity

Football fans immediately recognize the name of the head coach at Notre Dame University, perhaps the most highly visible football program in the world for the last 100 years. Under Bill Weis's coaching Notre Dame has fallen on hard times as I write these words, but the president of Notre Dame assures us that his coach is well worth his ten year contract of $35 million.

Coach Weis was interviewed on *60 Minutes* in the fall of 2006 and challenged with respect to the arrogance and brutality he exhibits with his players, particularly notable in the obnoxious language common to his vocabulary. He refers to it as "New Jersey language" and offers his four Super Bowl rings with the Giants and Patriots as evidence of his right to say what he wishes and treat players any way he deems appropriate. Says Weis, "When I'm not happy I make sure everyone around knows it." Regarding the Notre Dame football team, "I had to break them down before I could build them up. If you don't think you're good, then you have no chance." Does the public attention of alumni and outsiders to his behavior trouble the coach? Not at all, because "You only feel the pressure when you care about what someone else thinks." Despite Notre Dame's $61 million a year income from games, TV, and sports paraphernalia, Charlie Weis is, by any definition, a toxic leader.

I begin with that illustration to demonstrate that sometimes one cannot escape a toxic leader. Anyone who plays football for Notre Dame for the next eight years of Weis's contract can expect brutality on the practice field day after day. The president of Notre Dame, however, has not the slightest intention to interfere. He'll send the checks to the bank and offer a few extra "Hail Marys" for his obviously ungodly football coach.

In this book I have not yet talked about a leader's legacy, because so much of what we face with toxic leaders takes place in the present that we find it difficult to look at the future. But the word "legacy" increasingly creeps into the vocabulary of leadership books, notably in a recent book by James Kouzes and Barry Posner entitled *A Leader's Legacy*. That title offers something of a diving board from which we plunge into what their editor calls "a free flowing explanation of leadership topics and lessons" the authors have learned over the decades.[1] Nevertheless, they make every attempt to connect each of the 21 chapters to the central theme divided into four parts: significance, relationships, aspirations, and courage. The key message? "Legacy thinking means dedicating ourselves to *making a difference*, not just working to achieve fame and fortune. It also means appreciating that others will inherit what we leave behind."[2] The heart and soul of the book scream out against toxicity. People like Weis would always say "failure is not an option," Kouzes and Posner titled one of their chapters "Failure is Always an Option."

> Telling people that failure is not an option is just plain nonsense. Failure is always an option. In real life, when we're trying to do something we've never done before, we virtually never get it right the first time. And if we do, it's sheer luck. In real life, we make lots of mistakes when doing something new and different. In real life, failure is always an option. . . . But don't listen to us or an actor about greatness, listen instead to basketball legend Michael Jordan. One of the best ever to play the game, Jordan once observed, "I've missed more than 9,000 shots in my career, I've lost 300 games. Twenty-six times I've been trusted to take the winning shot and missed. I've failed over and over again in my life. And that is why I succeed."[3]

## Getting Rid Of Toxic Leaders

Obviously one solution to the problem, one that carries less penalty than assassination, suggests we just toss the toxic leader out of the organization. Baptists like to talk about "back door revival" when a congregation has improved because of people who leave the church. In the final analysis, since God cares about every individual (even a toxic leader), dismissal or resignation may not be the best answer. Nevertheless, it is an option we need to discuss.

---

1. Kouzes and Posner, *A Leader's Legacy*, 1.
2. Ibid., 5.
3. Ibid., 64.

## *Resisting Toxic Leadership*

After encouraging people to seize opportunity to take the lead, sharpen their own ideals, grasp the high ground and bond with others, Lipman-Blumen warns "Taken together, these opportunities can serve as boot camp for an organized revolt. On the other hand, organizing to overthrow a toxic leader can be quite risky. So resisters should think ahead to a fall back position or a workable exit strategy."[4] As the chapter ends she emphasizes that not everyone will want to be part of the revolt and "the right circumstances" are always essential.[5] Resistance will not work unless a reasonably large group of credible people are involved. They must be people who believe that leadership and true democracy is open to all and courage will be essential for anything you attempt against a toxic leader.

Kouzes and Posner claim that their research on the subject of courage indicates that "the leadership literature virtually ignores it."[6] They refer back to Socrates and Aristotle who "spoke of courage as the disposition that gives one the capacity to face danger without being overcome by fear. It's the capacity to persist under highly adverse circumstances. It's not about being fearless so much as it is to ability to control fear."[7]

## *Speaking Out*

Lipman-Blumen warns us not to consider speaking out on our own behalf a lesser good. She offers the much publicized case of Fred Korematsu vs. United States, a 22 year-old defense plant worker who refused to obey President Roosevelt's Executive Order 9066 which called for the interment of Japanese Americans during World War II.

> Although Korematsu acted initially for personal reasons, he saw the larger issue of injustice for people incarcerated simply on the basis of race. Eventually others who had been similarly harmed also benefited from Korematsu's courage. That initial injustice came from President Franklin D. Roosevelt, a leader whom historians have given high marks but whose decision in this case was clearly toxic.[8]

---

4. Lipman-Blumen, *The Allure of Toxic Leaders*, 196–97.
5. Ibid., 198.
6. Kouzes and Posner, *A Leader's Legacy*, 135.
7. Ibid., 136.
8. Lipman-Blumen, *The Allure of Toxic Leaders*, 205.

This calls up the courage issue once again. If the resistance group finds unity, its next step is to find a spokesman who can ironically present the case either to the toxic leader or to his or her superior. I like Ferguson's notion when he says

> Followers need to pray for the courage to kick their addictions to leaders with grand pie-in-the-sky visions, and look for leaders whose vision will inspire personal empowerment and improvement through hard work and honesty. . . . [Good leaders] see their leadership roles as vehicles of empowerment to promote authority and responsibility among those they lead.[9]

## Challenging the Vision

Research indicates that the bridge between a toxic leader and abused followers often arises from the leader's ability to depict an exciting and compelling vision for the future. Leadership literature almost always puts a positive spin on the word *vision* but one could correctly say that Osama bin Laden had an enormous vision for an attack on America; Adolf Hitler spoke repeatedly about his vision of the Third Reich conquering the world; and Lyndon Johnson promoted a futile vision to "free Viet Nam." Visions are not just descriptions of new products, new markets, and new sales goals. They might well carry a deadly toxicity and Lipman-Blumen claims that one can detect "the toxic seeds within the vision."

- Is the vision noble and positive for you and your group but detrimental to innocent others?
- Have multiple groups, with different needs, vetted these choices and subjected them to second and third opinions to determine whether there is benefit to most and harm to none or very few?
- Does the vision promise to make us large at the cost of making others small?
- Does the vision turn evil into moral virtue or moral virtue into human weakness?
- Does the vision involve the leader as the great savior who destroys your enemy or competitor?

---

9. Ferguson, "Stopping Toxic Leaders," 2.

- Does the vision require you to see others as enemies or tainted Others who must be ostracized or eradicated?[10]

These samples derive from her list, more than twice this long. Someone should speak out to neutralize a toxic leader. But the *time*, the *place*, and the *person addressed* as well as the *speaker* form absolutely crucial components of this maneuver.

Virtually every leader, from politician to pastor, stands in danger of looking for constant approval and therefore moving forward without considering conflicting information. Michael Roberto in his book *Why Great Leaders Don't Take Yes For An Answer* centers on promoting candor and building consensus from differing and conflicting viewpoints to reach effective action. He describes how *the decision making process develops throughout the organization, not just in the office of the CEO*. The trick requires promoting constructive conflict and preventing dysfunctional conflict.

Roberto feels that a majority of corporations have completely failed to achieve *decision quality* and *implementation effectiveness*. He claims that a leader's ability to navigate the personality clashes, politics and social pressures of the decision process often determines both of these. With clarity and conciseness he debunks common *myths* I have heard over and over again, even in the classroom.

- Only chief executives decide
- Decisions are made in the boss's office
- Decisions are primarily intellectual exercises
- Managers systematically analyze and then decide
- Managers decide and then act[11]

These all seem logical. In fact, they are all false to one degree or another, and the first may be the most foolish of all, especially for an organization committed to servant leadership. In defining the decision making process, Roberto points to four levels of power: composition, context, communication and control. Essentially they ask four questions:

1. Who participates?
2. What norms or ground rules control the deliberations?

---

10. Lipman-Blumen, 223–24.
11. Michael Roberto, 113.

3. How will information be exchanged among the leadership team members?
4. At what point will the chief leader introduce his or her own viewpoint?[12]

But how can we discern when conflict is constructive instead of dysfunctional? According to Roberto, constructive conflict produces interesting questions that provoke new lines of discovery and an attempt to understand the ideas of others. Dysfunctional conflict offers repetition of worn out arguments, turf guarding, and the loud voices of dominant leaders.

## *Considering the Replacement*

Assuming you have a group that meets all the qualifications identified so far in this chapter (employees, deacons, elders, parishioners), and have chosen your speaker and identified what he or she should say, to whom and when. You dare not put your resistance into operation until you have a suggested replacement. In my little handbook *Biblical Leadership* I include in the last chapter a section entitled "How Do You Spot a New Leader?" The paragraph may be worthy of reproduction here.

> Leaders must be constantly looking for capable people to train, mentor, and eventually turn over their leadership positions to them. So how do you spot potential for leadership? You look for a lot of things: *leadership in the past*, if possible. *Capacity to create or cast vision*. He or she doesn't have to be a visionary thinker but has to be able to get on the team and get with the forward motion. *A constructive spirit of discontent*. Leaders challenge the process. A spirit of discontent would be wrong; but a *constructive* spirit of discontent can be useful. *Practical ideas* that really work in the trenches. *Willingness to take responsibility*. We are an irresponsible society. We need to be responsible people, and we certainly need responsible leaders. *A finishing person*. In John 17 Jesus says, "Father, I am ready to come back to heaven because I have finished the work on earth which you have given me to do."[13]

Additional paragraphs go on to explain mental toughness, peer respect, family respect, a quality that causes people to listen, analysis of what this person will do to be liked, the presence of some destructive weakness,

---

12. Ibid., 222.
13. Gangel, *Biblical Leadership*, 102.

willingness to accept reasonable mistakes and whether "we can provide this new leader the environment he needs to succeed."[14]

Heifetz and Linsky, both of Harvard's Kennedy School of Government, suggest that the first criterion for a new leader is "the open heart."

> After years of raising questions and accumulating scars, most of us develop a set of defenses to protect ourselves. We buy into the common myth that you cannot survive a demanding leadership role without developing a thick skin. But that diminishes us, because it squeezes the juice out of our souls. We lose our capacity for innocence, curiosity, and compassion. In a sense, our hearts close—our innocence turns into cynicism, our curiosity turns into arrogance, and our compassion turns into callousness. We dress this up, of course, because we don't want to see ourselves—and certainly don't want others to see us—as cynical, arrogant, and calloused. We dress cynicism up as realism. So now we're not cynical; we're realistic. We are not arrogant, but we do have authoritative knowledge. And we dress up and cloak our callousness by calling it the thick skin of wisdom. But to stay alive in our spirits, in our hearts, requires the courage to keep our hearts open; it requires what Roman Catholics call a sacred heart or what in the Jewish tradition is called an open heart.[15]

## *Choosing Nontoxic Leaders*

The very last segment of Lipman-Blumen's book carries the title "Choosing the Nontoxic Leader." In the paragraphs that follow she pleads that we search for people with an even-handed attitude toward others, an insistence that we accept the *valuable inconvenience of leadership,* to search for the leader within, and select or elect people just a bit reluctant to take leadership. The last paragraph looks like this:

> Developing a complex understanding of our self and our world moves us further along this essential path to constructive, other-oriented leadership. Less driven by endless anxieties, over winning competitiveness, insatiable egos, endless needs for self-esteem, a pernicious achievement ethic, and calls to false heroics, we finally can assert our autonomy and set ourselves free. Then, through autonomy and freedom, we can find the inner strength not simply

---

14. Ibid., 103.
15. Heifetz and Linsky, "Leading With Open Heart," 30–31.

to escape, but to reject—resolutely and repeatedly—the allure of the toxic leader.[16]

## Getting Along with Toxic Leaders

For some readers, everything said in this chapter so far seems impossible. Perhaps the toxic leader is the founder or his son. Perhaps he or she owns the business or pastors with complete approval of the elders who, as a group, abuse the congregation. At any point, handing in one's resignation and leaving may look like the most desirable way to solve conflict. *It is not.* It may get you free from the battle, but it leaves all your abused companions exactly at the place from which you fled. Remember the statement above about finishing leadership. I have always advised my students to *never leave a ministry position or a church congregation unless they clearly understand God has finished with them in that place.* I remind you that the Apostle Paul considered suffering his greatest contribution to Christianity.

So assuming God gives you courage to endure, and believing He wants you to stay regardless of the difficulties and hurts you know still lie ahead, what essential steps can lead to *détente* with a toxic leader?

### *Learning*

In his new book *Unlearning Church*, Mike Slaughter talks about letting God live through you.

> Jesus, on his way to Jerusalem on the Sunday morning of the last week of his earthly life, met two blind beggars. They did not understand what Jesus was about to go through. They yelled out something to the effect of, "Jesus, Jesus, do you have anything left to give us?" It's amazing that Jesus was spiritually and emotionally available to stop and give himself for those folks. "Moved with compassion, Jesus touched their eyes. Immediately they regained their sight and followed him" (Matthew 20:34).
>
> As a leader do you ever feel you have nothing left to give? One night I was sitting in my house, having just returned from a trip out of town. It was the night before Ash Wednesday which is a big day at Ginghamsburg, and I was exhausted. The door bell rang at 9:20 pm. I said, "Who could possibly be at the door this late?" I opened the door and it was a senior in college whom Caroline and I have sponsored on missionary trips. He was planning to spend

---

16. Lipman-Blumen, 256.

a year on a mission in China. He wanted to talk. Inside I felt, "I don't feel like talking." But we welcomed him and heard his request for monthly support.

I felt like saying, "Go away!" But the secret of Christian life is not living out of what we feel but out of what we know and have experienced to be true.[17]

When you have identified a toxic leader, it quickly becomes easy to place all the blame on that person rather than asking God to open your own heart to essential changes and spiritual growth. Associate pastors who work with a toxic senior pastor for five years or more will incur bruises and cuts that may never disappear from their spirits. But every bruise and cut offers a learning experience which can draw that associate closer to God and make him or her more like Jesus Christ. That noble, notable goal should attract us even if we know we have to pass through long terms of agony to achieve it. Anyone can leave. *Learning how to use staying power presents a far greater challenge.*

## *Cooperation*

In "The Wrong Stuff" produced by FastCompany.com, Margaret Heffernan ponders the extent of toxicity in the business world.

> In talking to people about their work, it has been so hard to find people without at least one such negative experience that it's made me wonder how stomaching bullying is in our business environment. The lowest estimate says that 12% of workers are bullied; others put it as high 50%. Women are as likely as men to be toxic bosses—but women are 80% more likely to be the targets. Men pick on women—and women pick on women. The abused are neither young nor thin-skinned but tend to be in their forties, with years of experience behind them. And toxic bosses don't work alone—77% of them enlist others to help. So widespread is this phenomenon that lawyers seeking some legal remedy have found that in many cases, people see abuse and stress as simply intrinsic to employment.[18]

Since learning is the first step, one of the things we learn is *how to cooperate*. Sometimes people seem too young or inexperienced to function seriously in a leadership situation. But if you decide to cooperate with a known toxic leader, you dare not stop thinking creatively, allow your pro-

---

17. Slaughter, *Unlearning Church*, 208–9.
18. Heffernan, "The Wrong Stuff," 2.

ductivity to decline, or lose sight of the mission. Furthermore, cooperation does not mean allowing the toxic leader to lead you into unethical behavior or even corruption. Refusing to do something that you know is wrong in the sight of God may trigger your toxic boss to fire you. No it does not look good on your résumé, but God judges all things and He watches and protects the outcome of people who stand firm for righteousness.

### Detecting Early Signs of Toxicity

So much information now floats around about toxic leaders that you may start seeing things that do not exist. We do that well even in normal times, but after reading a book like this or Lipman-Blumen we can be easily spooked into thinking that everyone who disagrees with us is obviously a toxic leader. So we pause to consider the early signs of toxicity in a person or organization. Bacal suggests

> If you are a manager we suggest that if you find that there are some indications that your organization may becoming toxic, we urge you to look at yourself in an honest way. Remember that toxic organizations destroy people, and if you are developing a tendency toward toxic leadership, you will pay a huge price in terms of personal health and your career.[19]

But detecting early signs does not just refer to your analysis of other leaders, it refers to yourself as well.

### Finding Something Positive

Benjamin Franklin once wrote, "To pour forth benefits for the common good is divine." Walter Isaacson, in his book *Benjamin Franklin: An American Life* wrote

> "Compromisers may not make great heroes, but they do make democracies." He points out that the strength of country—or, I would argue, any organization—"is not just derived from singleness of purpose. It is derived from the recognition that the sum is greater than the parts and that compromise is often a necessary ingredient in achieving success."[20]

Krista Henley gives us hope for getting along with a toxic leader. "The old models of threat, order and hierarchy have been losing ground

---

19. Bacal, "Welcome to the Fire of an Unhealthy Workplace," 4.
20. Isaacson, *Benjamin Franklin: An American Life*, 32.

in favor of calibration and flat teams, in part because of long-term time demands. Yes, threats can work in the short term but long-range change requires support, encouragement, and a safe space for exploration of the past, and for creation of a new vision. Step by step coaching that honors the individual's experiences has been proven effective when confidentiality and respect are woven into the leadership development program."[21]

## *Depending Upon God*

Christians who serve under toxic leaders all come to the point, sometimes often, when they have nowhere to turn but the Heavenly Father. They live in a state of constant dependence, precisely where God wants all of us. Have a look at the following paragraph from *The Message*.

> Since God has so generously let us in on what he is doing, we are not about to throw up our hands and walk off the job just because we run into occasional hard times. We refuse to wear masks and play games. We don't maneuver and manipulate behind the scenes. And we don't twist God's Word to suit ourselves. Rather, we keep everything we do and say out in the open, the whole trust on display, so that those who want to can see and judge for themselves in the presence of God (2 Cor 4:1–2).[22]

# Retuning the Organization

Most experts agree that a toxic leader poisons the entire organization and major changes must take place even if he or she leaves. For example, we are forced to ask, "How do we avoid ever appointing a toxic leader again?" Have we overlooked tricks of the trade that can help us purify our churches and organizations after they have been poisoned by a toxic leader? The answer is yes, and we will look at five.

One of the boards of which I have been a member in the past has a clear constitutional statement about term limits—three-three year terms for a total of nine. I noticed during my years of service that no one seemed to leave the board. Instead, as the issue came up at one board meeting and the board discovered if they implemented this policy five authoritative and vocal members would have to leave at the same time, they simply decided to disregard the provision. When my nine years concluded, I handed in my resignation not just because it was the *right* thing to do, but because it

---

21. Henley, "Detoxifying a Toxic Leader," 2.
22. Peterson, *The Message*, 373.

was the *legal* thing to do. I have heard the CEO of that organization declare to one of its accountability bodies that the board would reform and begin adhering to that policy immediately. That occurred approximately five years before my resignation and I saw no evidence that promise was ever kept.

Strict term limits, especially on boards and committees, can do a great deal of good in keeping toxic leaders out of control. Let's hear from Lipman-Blumen again:

> The processes by which we select and keep leaders in public and private office often attract the wrong candidate for the wrong reasons. Thomas Jefferson described his perspective on the danger this way: "Whenever a man has cast a longing eye on offices, a rottenness begins in his conduct." And even when leaders enter with respectable levels of competence and integrity, many remain in office so long that they eventually reach their level of incompetence. The result is that they dwindle into mediocrity or worse. And, of course, Lord Actin's famous dictum applies here as well, since long terms of office tend to concentrate inordinately the leader's power: "Power tends to corrupt, and absolute power corrupts absolutely." In fact, it is virtually a truism that even nontoxic leaders who hang on too long commonly go from good to bad.[23]

I have spoken to this in an earlier chapter because, as with all large problems, we best face them head on as early as possible. Churches have earned notoriety for knowing too little about pastors they call. I have been on both sides of the interviewing process, and on one or two occasions I found myself asking some 80% of the questions, even questions that should certainly have been addressed to me. Here's a simple example. Churches often ask a new pastor to explain his vision for the church. Of all the ridiculous questions I have heard, this could be the worst. Before the committee sits a man who has never been to this town before, has pastored a different church in a different place with different people for the past eight years, and we want him in five minutes to articulate where he thinks our church should be going over the next five years?

When asked that question I don't even attempt an answer. I simply turn the question around and ask, "What is *your* vision for *your* church for the near future?" Along this line as well we must make very sure the search committee or the group examining candidates for leadership work their way through to the truth.

---

23. Lipman-Blumen, 213–14.

Since this book flows so directly from Lipman-Blumen, let me offer her own definition of this crucial four word sentence.

> Many leaders cling to the role because they can't bear giving up the comfortable perks that leaders usually enjoy. When we let leaders remain in office too long, we also stifle the talents, ingenuity, and enthusiasm of other leaders with fresh ideas. We also block the emergence of younger generations of leaders waiting in the wings. So we need to develop respectable exit options.[24]

Colleges have done rather well on this with their plethora of titles such as chancellors, professors emeriti, and other offices that allow faculty or administrators to stay hooked up to the college even after retiring. Churches struggle at thinking through this option but veteran pastors have much to offer through international ministries, ministering to the elderly, and serving branch churches.

Earlier in the book we learned from the Eli story that holy men hold the church's reputation in their hands. God has little interest in our excuses, yet we seem to concoct them with ease.

Irresponsible parents produce irresponsible children, and the fact that Eli was a priest cut him no slack with God. *Pastors should answer to elder boards, not rule them.* At the very most their title (a gift not an office) makes them leaders among leaders with the elder board. Churches utilizing the deacon construction can make the same plan work. *The most vulnerable type of toxicity for a congregation arises from an all powerful pastor who reigns over all boards and committees and the congregation.*

We could do no better than end our book by coming to the words of Kouzes and Posner in the "Afterword" of *A Leader's Legacy*.

> Legacies aren't the results of wishful thinking. They are the result of determined doing. The legacy you leave is the life you lead. We lead our lives daily. We leave our legacy daily. The people you see, the decisions you make, the actions you take—they are what tell your story. It's the sum of everything you do that matters, not one large bequest at the end of your tenure. Despite all our talk about leaders needing to be concerned about the future, the most important leadership actions are the ones you take today.
>
> You just never know whose life you might touch. You just never know what change you might initiate and what . . .[25]

---

24. Ibid., 215.
25. Kouzes and Posner, *The Leaders' Legacy*, 180.

# Bibliography

Anderson, J. Kirby. *Moral Dilemmas*. Waco: Word, 1998.
Anderson, Leith. *Dying for Change*. Minneapolis: Bethany House, 1990.
———. *Leadership That Works*. Minneapolis: Bethany House, 1999.
Bacal, Robert. "Welcome to the Fire of an Unhealthy Workplace," Internet Essay on Conflict 991.com 1, 2000.
Beers, V. Gilbert. *The Victor Handbook of Bible Knowledge*. Wheaton: Victor Books, 1981.
Bennis, Warren. *Why Leaders Can't Lead*. San Francisco: Jossey-Bass, 1989.
Blanchard, Ken and Associates. *Leading at a Higher Level*. Upper Saddle River, NJ: Prentiss-Hall. 2007.
Bornstein, Steven M. and Anthony F. Smith. "The Leader Who Serves." *The Leader of the Future,* F. Hesselbein, M. Goldsmith, R. Beckard, and R. Schubert, editors. San Francisco: Jossey-Bass, 1998.
Branham, Leigh. *The 7 Reasons Employees Leave*. New York: AMACOM, 2005.
Chafer, Lewis Sperry. *He That is Spiritual*. Grand Rapids: Zondervan, (Rev. edition, 1967).
Chandler, Steve and Duane Black. *The Hands-Off Manager*. Franklin Lakes, NJ: The Career Press, 2007.
Chenoweth, Dan. "Five Characteristics That Separate Great Leaders from Toxic Leaders." www.expertmagazine.com (November, 2005).
Collins, Jim. *Good to Great*. New York: Harper Business, 2001.
Dotlich, David L. and Peter C. Cairo. *Unnatural Leadership*. San Francisco: Wiley, 2002.
Ferguson, Vincent L. "Stopping Toxic Leaders" *The Bahama News,* www.jonesbahamas.com (October 16, 2006).
Finch, Miles. "Surprised By Pride." *Leadership* (Spring, 2007).
Finzel, Hans. *The Top Ten Mistakes Leaders Make*. Colorado Springs: NEXGEN, 2000 revision.
Gangel, Kenneth O. *Biblical Leadership*. Evangelical Training Association, 2007.
———. *Coaching Ministry Teams*. Eugene, OR: Wipf and Stock, 2006.
———. "Joshua" *Old Testament Commentary*. Nashville: Broadman & Holman, 2003.
Gangel, Kenneth O. and Steven J. Bramer. "Genesis" *Old Testament Commentary,* Nashville: Broadman & Holman, 2002.
George, Bill with Peter Sims. *True North*. San Francisco: Jossey-Bass, 2007.
Goldsmith, Marshall and Kelley. "Helping People Establish Their Goals" *Leader to Leader* (Winter, 2006).
Goffee, Rob and Gareth Jones. "Leading Clever People." *Harvard Business Review* (March, 2007).
———. *Why Should Anyone Be Led By You?* Boston: Harvard Business School Press, 2006.
Halpin, Andrew W. *Theory and Research in Administration*. New York: McMillan, 1966.
Heffernan, Margaret. "The Wrong Stuff." www.fastcompany.com/resources/columnists/mh/041204.html. 10/30/2006.

## Bibliography

Heifetz, Ronald A and Marty Linsky. "Leading With An Open Heart." *Leader to Leader,* No. 26 (Fall 2002)

Hendrix, Olan. *Three Dimensions of Leadership.* St. Charles, IL: ChurchSmart, 2000.

Henley, Krista. "Detoxifying a Toxic Leader" *Innovative Leader* Vol. 12, No. 6 (June, 2003).

Hunter, James C. *The World's Most Powerful Principle.* New York: Crown Business, 2004.

Huntsman, Jon M. *Winners Never Cheat.* Upper Saddle River, NJ: Wharton School Publishing, 2005.

Jakes, T. D. *The Ten Commandments of Working in a Hostile Environment.* Berkley, CA: Berkley Press, 2005.

Kanter, Rosabeth Moss. "How Leaders Gain (and Lose) Confidence." *Leader to Leader* (Winter, 2005).

—————. *Confidence.* New York: Crown Business, 2004.

Katzenbach, Jon R. and Douglas K. Smith, "The Discipline of Teams." *Harvard Business Review* (July 2005).

Kellerman, Barbara. "How Bad Leadership Happens." *Leader to Leader* (Winter, 2005).

Kouzes, James M. and Barry L. Posner. *A Leader's Legacy.* San Francisco: Jossey-Bass, 2006.

Kramer, Roderick M. "The Great Intimidators." *Harvard Business Review* (February, 2006).

Lencioni, Patrick. *The Three Signs of a Miserable Job.* San Francisco: Wiley, 2007.

Lipman-Blumen, Jean. *The Allure of Toxic Leaders: Why We Follow Destructive Bosses and Corrupt Politicians—And How We Can Survive Them.* New York: Oxford University Press, 2005.

—————. "Toxic Leadership: When Grand Illusions Masquerade as Noble Visions." *Leader to Leader* (Spring, 2005).

Liechty, Daniel. http://staff.washington.edu/nelgee/hidden/hidn_5.htm. 10/16/2006.

Lencioni, Patrick. *The Five Temptations of a CEO,* San Francisco: Jossey-Bass, 1998.

Maxwell, John C. *Talent Is Never Enough.* Nashville: Thomas Nelson, 2007.

Otazo, Karen. *The Truth about Being a Leader.* Upper Saddle River, NJ: FT Press, 2007.

Peterson, Eugene H. *The Message: The Bible in Contemporary Language.* Colorado Springs, CO: NAVPRESS, 2002.

Pyne, Robert A. *Humanity and Sin.* Nashville: Word Publishing, 1999.

Roberto, Michael. *Why Great Leaders Don't Take Yes For An Answer.* Upper Saddle River, NJ: Wharton School Publishing, 2005.

Rock, David. *Quiet Leadership.* New York: Collins, 2006.

Schaeffer, Francis A. *True Spirituality.* Wheaton, IL: Tyndale House, 1972.

Senge, Peter. "Missing the Boat on Leadership." *Leader to Leader.* Fall 2005 no. 38.

Sheppard, Blair and Joel Leboeuf. "Leadership Development Needs of the Business World." *Leader to Leader* (2006).

Shetty, Hari. "Organization Environment To Defuse Toxic Leadership" www.cio.com/archive/041506/leadership.html. May 11, 2006.

Sitkin, Sim B., E. Allan Lynn and Sanyin Siang. "The Six Domains of Leadership." *Leader to Leader* (2007).

Spears, Larry C. "Practicing Servant-Leadership" *Leader to Leader* No. 34 (Fall 2004).

Tracy, Brian. *Crunch Point.* New York: AMACON, 2007.

Turknett, Robert L. and Caroline N. *Descent People, Descent Company.* Mountain View, CA: Davies-Black, 2005.

Whicker, Marsha Lynn. *When Organizations Go Bad*, Greenwood: Quoram Books. 1996.

*Bibliography*

Ulrich, Dave. "Credibility X Capability" *Leader of the Future*, ed. Francis Hesselbein, Marshall Goldsmith and Richard Beckhard. San Francisco: Jossey-Bass, 1996.

Useem, Michael. "How Well-Run Boards Make Decisions." *Harvard Business Review* (November, 2006).

Made in the USA
San Bernardino, CA
14 May 2019